Religion for a Dislocated Generation

Where will those who grew up in the sixties find faith?

Barbara Hargrove

Judson Press ® Valley Forge

Religion for a Dislocated Generation

Copyright © 1980
Judson Press, Valley Forge, PA 19481

All rights reserved. No part of this publication may be reproduced, stored in a retrieval system, or transmitted in any form or by any means, electronic, mechanical, photocopying, recording, or otherwise, without the prior permission of the copyright owner, except for brief quotations included in a review of the book.

Library of Congress Cataloging in Publication Data

Hargrove, Barbara W.
   Religion for a dislocated generation.

   1. Young adults—United States—Religious life. 2. United States—Religion—1960-   3. United States—Civilization—1945-   I. Title.
BL2530.U6H37   291'.0973   80-25400
ISBN 0-8170-0891-8

The name JUDSON PRESS is registered as a trademark in the U.S. Patent Office. Printed in the U.S.A. ⊕

*To my children and their children,
that our dislocation may find
resolution in a new vision of hope.*

Acknowledgments

It is always impossible to give proper credit to all those who have helped one put together a book. This book was written as a result of responses to an unpublished monograph detailing research I had done during the 1972–1973 academic year, under a grant by the National Endowment for the Humanities, with the New Religious Consciousness project at Berkeley. That project, headed by Charles Glock and Robert Bellah, was located in the Survey Research Center of the University of California, with ties to that university's Department of Sociology and the Graduate Theological Union of Berkeley. I am greatly indebted to the project team and its leaders, as well as to all those in youth and campus ministry whom I interviewed for my part of the project and those I contacted again during my follow-up study in 1978, funded by the National Institute for Campus Ministries.

The roots of my interest and indebtedness go back further, to my students, my children, and their friends, particularly the denizens of what came to be known as "Mama-San's Boarding House." It was largely their concerns that sent me to Berkeley to find the roots of the counterculture in the first place.

More recently, I must thank Hal Viehman for his interest in the original monograph, and Harold Twiss for encouraging this product. Bot Pote, my student assistant, has given valuable time and effort reading the manuscript and offering suggestions. The administration of Iliff School of Theology, particularly by asking me to speak on this subject at the Iliff Week of Lectures, gave me impetus to carry through the project.

Beyond these specifics, the field widens. This book comes out of experiences of a lifetime, sociological perspectives of an entire education, far more books than those specifically cited here, contacts with colleagues, students, and friends, all of whom are in some way present in these pages.

Denver, Colorado
April, 1980

Contents

Chapters
1. The Great Migration of World War II 9
2. Education for a Dislocated Generation 31
3. Religion for a Dislocated Generation 65
4. A Unique Cohort? 89
5. Religion, the Church, and Modern Society 113
Notes 137

Chapter 1

The Great Migration of World War II

The generation that is now assuming positions of responsibility in American society has been of special interest throughout its life. This particular age cohort comprises the post-World War II baby boom, and hence it is significant if only because of its sheer numbers. These are the children who never knew a classroom that was not overcrowded, who went through school during the post-Sputnik push for technological and scientific excellence, who faced being called to fight a meaningless war in Vietnam, and who reached the age of public responsibility just in time for Watergate. If there has indeed been a major cultural break in this century, this particular age cohort must stand astride it. They, more than any other group, may be the shapers of the future as it opens before us.

Margaret Mead, at a time when this group was college age, wrote of the need for them to assume leadership in an age in which their elders were cultural immigrants, unable to be sure of their own direction, much less to guide their offspring.¹ But unlike the earlier shapers of the culture, these young people were products of a secular age which did not posit ultimate goals and values, but rather cast all knowledge in relative terms. The Judeo-Christian tradition may celebrate the faith of Abraham, who went out from Haran not knowing where he was going. However, his faith also posited a God who would guide and sustain him. Among these twentieth-century wanderers we have found in one study over one-fourth who either believed in no God, were unsure about it, or could only say that they thought there must be something "more" or "beyond." Faced with traditional cultural modes of understanding life, one-sixth of these young people were found to trust only their own inner subjective experience as a basis for their meaning system.² Surely they are wanderers in a wasteland, these people to whom some would have us turn for guidance!

The plethora of new religious movements which have arisen in the past decade or more may well reflect the search within this age group for some kind of ultimate grounding no longer available to them through established social institutions. It may also indicate an equally serious search among other age groups for whom the people in question have proved blind leaders of the blind. Established religious institutions that have in the past both legitimated and helped guide the American experiment are faced with the need to redefine the cultural task in the light of their understanding of the divine mandate, or else must face the charge of irrelevancy in a society that claims to have outgrown their vision.

This book, then, is an attempt to understand some of the antecedents of this unique age cohort, to test whether they do or do not stand at the edge of some major cultural break, and to assess the reciprocal effects of their experiences and some of the major institutions of the society, particularly that of religion. For if indeed we are at some new point in culture, we will find that some kind of grounding in ultimate meaning is called for, whether or not it is found in current religious institutions.

The Roots of Dislocation

While the experiences of the generation now in their twenties and thirties in America are in many ways unique, the experience of uprootedness or dislocation has been an important factor in the development of American culture. Early settlers pulled up their European roots to seek a new place in the New World; and as they found that place, they uprooted and pushed back the native Americans whose culture they ignored. Out of the settlements on the eastern coast new generations of migrants pulled loose to expand the frontier farther and farther west. Blacks brought to these shores against their will were, like the Native Americans, assumed to have no culture of their own and were separated totally from the patterns and communities that had formed them. Later waves of immigrants from northern, southern, and eastern Europe, from China, Japan, India, the Middle East, and most recently from southeast Asia and Latin America, have successively been torn from their cultural roots and expected to become part of the great American experiment.

Yet it is my contention that in some respects the internal dislocation that took place in this country around the time of the Second World War was more severe and had greater consequences to the society than any of those previous uprootings. For one thing, the idea of the "American experiment" carries with it the implicit assumption of some sort of common task, in which the people were forming a culture out of the disparate influences brought here by all those uprooted immigrants, or were extending that culture over a broader and broader geographic area. Admitted, the first people to move out into any new area are likely to be cultural mavericks, driven at least as much by their distaste for settled ways as by their desire to spread those ways. The whalers, mountain men, trappers, cowboys, railroad men, traders, and the like were scarcely what we usually mean when we speak of "civilizing influences." But they were soon followed by family folk, missionaries, and others who did see their task as a cultural one.

For most, the basis of the new culture was economic. The call of new lands, the challenge of economic development, appealed first of all to individuals and families, but there was also an underlying assumption that what benefited one would benefit all. And the products of the work of each would go to the establishment of a way of life richer, freer, more whole than humankind had yet achieved.

For many, the vision was also a religious one. The rhetoric of American civil religion claimed America to be God's New Israel, where humankind might again be given the example of the new order intended by the Creator, where one should be able to rest under one's own vine and fig tree, where leaders understood themselves to be servants of the people and of a God who demanded justice and an upright way of life. Basic to that idea was the kind of theology that was emphasized in the Protestant Reformation, where it was felt that God was served in the common vocations of the people. So pervasive had this "Protestant Ethic" become that it had also become a basic assumption of many whose backgrounds were far from Protestant Christianity. In essence, it legitimated the great experiment, giving it ultimate as well as proximate value, making America that city set on a hill to which all nations might look for inspiration and guidance.

By the first quarter of the twentieth century, American culture appeared to have reached a point of stability. It is not that life was static; the culture was one of a bustling, highly mobile society in which change—defined as progress—was taken for granted. Commerce dominated the society, promising the goods for an ever-improving style of life that extended to all social classes. Nearly everyone seemed to believe the stories of Horatio Alger and others that celebrated the opportunity of anyone who truly tried to mount the ladder of success.

That ladder was taken for granted, and the definition of success was fairly clear. As Oscar Handlin has noted, the early assumptions about American culture being the mutual product of all elements in the melting pot had been replaced by a fixed idea of the American character as a mold into which any new elements must be formed.[3] The model was dominated by a middle-class tradition, but for most people life tended to be bounded by the neighborhood or social class into which they were born. Ideas of change and progress were fitted into the picture by methods of child rearing that, instead of training into explicit behavior as is common in traditional societies, inculcated a kind of generalized sense of direction—what David Riesman called an "inner gyroscope." In this way young people were guided by parents and teachers to transcend their current ideas and patterns of living, with the direction of transcendence clearly provided.[4] For most young people, that meant growing up in a stable neighborhood where values and morals were fairly well shared by all those with whom they came into close contact. It also meant going through a period of rebellion against the apparent narrowness of that environment in order to move out into some broader arena for the exercise of their talents. These new arenas, however, seldom represented a severe disjunction with their background environment, since they had already been partially perceived by their guiding elders and were populated by others who had arrived there by routes similar to their own. Young people, for example, were expected to reach higher levels of education than their elders had, which would then allow them to take positions where they would deal with a broader range of people and activities. Or they were expected to leave the family farm and move to a nearby city, exchange blue collars for white, or move from clerical to professional work. In each case it was assumed that the skills, the attitudes, and the social graces they had learned at home or in school would provide a foundation for an improved life. They might need further cultivation, often through facing ridicule, exhausting effort, or considerable hardship, but effort and the facing of hardship were often seen as elements in the normative American character of the time.

Most Americans in those days lived in an environment most nearly represented by the term "small town." If they lived on farms, they tended to have involvements in schools and churches of the nearest town. If they lived in cities, they tended to stay within the neighborhood they shared with their own social class or ethnic group. Even if they were rich enough to travel and to have separate summer and winter homes, they still tended to spend nearly all their time with members of the same set, oblivious to the style of life of others who may have lived not too far away.

In each particular neighborhood or class, then, patterns of responsible behavior and directions of mobility might be somewhat different, but they all tended to be aimed at that group's definition of the good life or of the life-style immediately above it on the ladder of mobility.

While business was the primary definer of success, and the school its principal avenue, the church was often its legitimator, though sometimes in ways not of its own choosing. Most of the small towns and bounded neighborhoods clustered around one or more churches, temples, or synagogues, where the style of life of the people, their goals, and their values were set in the context of ultimate concerns. Here children were taught stories of heroes of their faith, whose lives offered examples of appropriate behavior and motivation. Here they learned that the ways they were told to behave had divine sanction. Here they found an extension of the family in which they were loved, cared for, scolded, and nurtured, where they found most of their friends and quite often their mates as well. Here, as has been true in most religions, they not only were shaped into moral beings but also were taught to envision a more perfect life than that which they could see around them. Some of those visions were the substance of their revolt against the home community, and often they revolted as well against the churches which had engendered their hope.

Sometimes the move out of the old neighborhood meant a change to a different denomination as well as to a different congregation, as the poor young person worked up the ladder to middle-class status and rejected the sectarian worship of his or her origins. One way to establish oneself as successful was to become a member of a congregation of the successful and to have one's children learn in this new religious environment that God had willed a morality appropriate to this higher station.

But for all the changing, people tended to stay within general denominational or faith boundaries. Protestants still were suspicious of Catholicism, and Catholics were warned against Protestants. Jews were even more separate, forming instead their own internal denominations. In most cases, religious proof of mobility was found within the denomination, by moving from one congregation to another of higher status, with a newer building, a better location, a more affluent membership.

There was in general a sense of the separateness of different categories of people, whether on the basis of religion, politics, social class, or race. Democrats really did not know how Republicans could think the way they did, and one tended to receive one's political party by inheritance as one did religion. South and North were separate cultures, neither sure that the other was really moral. Blacks and whites, poor and rich, ethnic groups of all sorts, all seemed to live in separate worlds. City and country applied their own standards of judgment against one another. And yet each one of these separate groups was secure in its understanding of itself as American, and each individual was likely to have enough overlapping loyalties to have interests in the welfare of several categories of people. It was a strange mixture of separation and unity, of conflict and consensus. But for most of the people the society seemed to have a recognizable pattern, a direction of movement, and a place for everyone—this last to be earned by personal effort. Two forms of judgment were reserved for those who seemed to have no place: Either they were on the way to finding their spot, or, if not, they were somehow less than human. In all too many cases, even the outsiders came to agree with this evaluation of their worth, with consequences ranging from massive efforts to fit some mold, to total surrender of their sense of personhood.

Even the Great Depression did not fully shake people's confidence in the social pattern, though there were those whose hold on a place in the society was weakened by unemployment and forced migration. But nearly everyone understood this to be a temporary setback and knew that we had lived through those problems before. The criticisms of those who blamed the system, who claimed that something could be done about changing the state of the outcast, received little notice. They seemed to be rebelling against that which was simply the nature of American life.

The Effects of World War II

It was World War II that really shook the foundations, and the first cause of that shaking was the draft. This was not the first war for which citizens had been drafted. Lincoln had been impelled to draft soldiers for the Union army in the Civil War. But draftees could hire someone to take their place in the service; so that the men who actually went were either those who were inclined toward wartime adventure or committed to the cause, or the poor who could not hire a replacement or were willing to take the pay to become one. In World War I the paid replacement was no longer available to the draftee, but there were ample provisions for the deferment of married men or those engaged in farming or industry in any way related to the war effort. So again the war siphoned off a relatively small proportion of young men, most of them single, with class distinctions fairly well maintained by the separation of officers from enlisted men. For many, also, the period of wartime service was relatively short.

The draft of World War II was far more universal, and it lasted much longer. It cut a wide swath, requiring service of married men, defining job deferments quite strictly. Then, too, it was a war of expanding technology, where men who managed to get certain kinds of training were catapulted into leadership regardless of their social background. (A symptom of the rapidity of advancement in certain fields was the variety of jokes in the air force about problems of serving liquor to lieutenant colonels who were under drinking age.) At the same time, college men without technical training were often drafted into the lowest ranks, where one might find within a single platoon an Ivy League graduate, a farm boy, a mountain moonshiner, and the son of an immigrant miner. The draft was nationwide; National Guard units formed from particular localities or states were swallowed up in an army of draftees who were brought together from East and West, North and

South, city and country. Only in the matter of race was the separation maintained, and by the end of the war that too had begun to go. The one place that the separation held was in the matter of sex; only a few women participated in the armed services, and they were kept segregated.

The men, called from their separate communities, were brought together under circumstances that often required sharing close quarters, depending for their very lives upon one another, and sharing experiences often so disturbing that they would never be able to relate them to members of their family or their neighbors.

Another effect of military service was the disturbance of that inner gyroscope developed in the inner-directed young of the earlier period. The kind of unidirectional pattern of life it served no longer was part of the experience of many who served in the armed forces. Hard work did not bring success; often the one who coped most successfully was the company "goldbrick," the one who found ways to avoid work. To volunteer for duty did not bring rewards; it only brought more duty, often of a meaningless or dangerous kind. People only made fun of the "eager beaver." Boys who had grown up on stories of World War I flying aces and joined the air force found themselves at the panels of huge bombers, flying high above enemy action, dropping bombs on distant targets that they must think of impersonally for their own peace of mind. Engagement with the enemy was not heroic; it was boring, demeaning, and occasional. The "old army game" was primarily a round of occasions to "hurry up and wait." There was no place for the entrepreneur—at least, not for the honest one. And the particular goals one had learned at home as almost universal truths often were far different from those of people who had become trusted comrades. Men began to question many of the basic assumptions of their families and communities in the face of a wide range of alternatives that often appeared to have little semblance to those earlier ideas, and yet served as guideposts in the lives of people with whom they now shared a common existence.

It mattered, too, that these experiences extended into year

after weary year, until it became difficult even to remember the world view that still informed those letters from home. But it was also important that for a high percentage of these men the end of the war did not mean a return to the home community and the old job. Rather, they found that the technological advances spurred by the war had opened up seemingly unlimited new opportunities at home—opportunities the government was willing to help them prepare for through higher education under the GI Bill.

So they poured into the universities and technical schools of the country, ready to prepare for a new life. Already uprooted from home communities, they were free to find the college that offered what they most wanted, or one which had room for them or a chance of employment for their wives, or was in a part of the country they had liked when they were stationed there, or where buddies were going to be. Schools put up villages of "temporary" housing and classrooms to make room for the influx, and men uprooted wives and families from home communities, or they brought brides they had found during their military travels, or they married local girls and settled down to study and to reenter civilian life. For many the Quonset hut or prefab apartment on campus was the first home of their own they had ever had. For others it was a long step down from officers' quarters on military bases, from an officer's salary to the GI allowance, compounded by the trauma of finding that the GI allowance was larger than any salary the returnee could command with his past civilian training. For the student veterans, this shock was mitigated by their new student role, but for wives who had often moved directly from high school to officers' quarters, it was a disaster.

The process was also a problem for wives in ways we are only now beginning to realize. One of the patterns that had begun to develop in that older and more settled time was a cultural division of labor between men and women in which the women of the working and middle classes tended often to be better educated than the men. Boys tended to go to school only until they were strong enough to take a man's place at work or until they had finished high school or trade school if that would help them find a job. Girls, however, often stayed on in school until the boys their age were settled enough in jobs to be able to afford marriage. Girls trained to be teachers "just in case" or at least learned enough of the finer things in life to be able to point their families toward a more refined life-style. A significant segment of the women stayed on to become scholars and professionals. There was a kind of trade-off by which the men had economic and political power and the women were the cultural leaders of family and community. With the GI Bill, women lost this advantage. It was the men who continued in the classroom, while the women often took relatively unskilled jobs to help with finances during this period. For the time their husbands were students, they may have exercised some economic power as the family breadwinner; but in the long run they tended to lose all leadership in the family and, with migration, in the community as well. When the men graduated, everyone wanted to return to the old patterns of stable family life, but in some ways the women were no longer equipped to find in their roles personal satisfaction or a sense of self-worth.

The Building of Suburbia

Of course, not everyone was drafted, and not everyone who went into military service returned to go to college. In fact, during the war years a kind of societal "fruit basket upset" game was being played in the civilian population as well. The technology of war that had been the occasion for the breakdown of social patterns in the military had also prompted vast migrations of civilian workers to defense plants in urban areas, had brought about widespread employment of women in heavy industry, and had been the occasion of a major shift of the black population out of the South. All these factors would become part of the evolving nature of the postwar society, and all of them tended to repeat the military pattern of uprooting from home communities followed by close contact among people who represented a wide variety of the many distinct lifestyles that had made up American culture.

During the war many of these workers had earned more

money than they had ever imagined they could, and many had received on-the-job training that would allow them to continue to climb the occupational ladder. Wartime shortages of consumer goods and housing had enforced saving, and when the war was over, these workers were among the first to stimulate the housing boom. Most were not city people by background, but had been crowded into urban centers where the defense plants were located. The jobs were still there, but now they had a chance to indulge their longing for a home of their own, with its own little piece of land where they could have the lawns and gardens they had left behind, and where their children might play safely in fresh air on quiet streets like those of the old hometowns. But these were no longer the small towns of their youth. For one thing, the towns kept growing as more and more workers moved out of the city and were joined by the college men as they finished their degrees and came to the metropolis for jobs. In addition, they lacked individuality. These towns could not harken back to the personal histories of founding families who had settled there and slowly built up patterns of shared lives. Their founders were corporate land developers, who put up a subdivision the size of a small city in a brief period of time and then moved on to some new location. The people who moved in by the hundreds within weeks of one another had no common histories other than the general history of uprooting. One's neighbor on one side may have come from the Deep South; on the other side might be a family of second generation immigrants. The patterns of family life, the goals and aspirations, the very rhythms of activity of each household might be poles apart. The one thing they did have in common was an income that would allow the purchase of a house in this subdivision, where all houses were approximately the same price, and a family that fit here, where houses were nearly all the same size.

For many occupants of those houses their current income and status were far beyond anything that their families' socialization could have prepared them for, and their employment was associated with life-styles far different from those they had known. They were, in many cases, clusters of people left almost without a culture, caught up in a dizzying rush of economic expansion that pushed them to change, rather than being called ahead to change by some vision of the good life such as had led their forebears to settle the land. The purveyors of the good life were now the advertisers of consumer goods, who appealed to them as individuals and families, rather than dreamers of dreams of some corporate goal. The family—the independent nuclear unit of father, mother, and minor children—became the basic and often the only unit of the society. No longer were extended families, neighborhoods, and communities intermediaries between this unit and the wider world. Faced directly with the large and often baffling world of suburbia and metropolis, families closed ranks in self-defense, and "togetherness" was born. Attempting to clarify the rungs on a newly complicated ladder of success, people found status among their neighbors through patterns of family consumption. Houses all alike must bear marks of improvement; the car in the garage must be new and newly polished; the backyard must sport a patio and grill; the children must have special lessons and possessions.

The critics of the 1950s developed terms for what was going on. William H. Whyte wrote of the "organization man," for whom the Protestant Ethic had been replaced by the "social ethic," individual initiative by the desire to make it to the top by getting along with others and following the rules. David Riesman wrote of the exchange of the gyroscope of the "inner-directed" for a kind of interpersonal radar of the "other-directed." "The man in the gray flannel suit" became the object of criticism, if not pity, as he forced himself through years of the rat race to maintain a family in suburbia.[5]

But there was no going back. A quick visit to the old hometown or the family farm would show that. Back on the farm, the men who had managed to avoid the draft with agricultural deferments had been joined by returning military men getting a start with government aid, and both had made great economic leaps in the postwar expansion of agriculture. The expansion required new technology in production and marketing, a new and essentially urban frame of mind. Farming as a way of life retreated before agribusiness, and farmers, needing more land to utilize their new machines efficiently, bought up the necessary acres from others who had migrated to urban areas. Small towns faced with this new kind of business either expanded and brought in new services and new kinds of people to manage them or faded away as the agribusinessmen passed them by on the new highways that led to larger centers of trade.

Small-town people who had followed national news during the war period out of concern for loved ones who served overseas found that they were now committed to a national view of public events rather than a local focus. National media replaced the local small-town newspaper—and local gossip—as the primary source of news. And national media in their interpretation of events and advertisements offered a view of life that was essentially urban, oriented to the particular pattern of mobility that was concentrated in commercial centers.

People for whom the old patterns no longer made sense turned to media-fostered definitions of American culture. Families depicted on TV lived in suburbia and were happy there. They made use of all the products advertised as necessary for a genuine American existence. In many cases people learned from such TV fiction the patterns of behavior, the expected attitudes, and standards for their new life-style. No matter what their original background, neighbors could share these models and so could have something on which to build a common universe.

Both the economic structure and the mobility of the population supported the shift of all types of communications media from a local to a national focus. Commercial success of media demanded an ever-expanding clientele, one that must not be offended by narrow parochialisms of any component group. Local newspapers that had interpreted the world through the lenses of a particular local, ethnic, or class constituency began to lose their power to centralized and broadly based urban news organizations whose corporate structures made their primary concern the bottom line of profit rather than the expression of the viewpoint of a particular audience.

Local radio stations gave way to national networks, and television developed as an even more centralized medium.

All these forms of communication came directly into the home, no longer mediated by local associations. Commercial firms, as they sponsored network shows and advertised in the larger newspapers and magazines, envisioned a national market which must not be offended. Political considerations, as World War II was followed by the cold war, demanded the continuation of a sense of identification with national rather than local concerns. The particular opinions of any group or class could remain acceptable only as long as they did not weaken the national consensus, political or economic. Even local governmental units must yield to the larger political considerations of the national government, interpreted by the national media and centralized boards. Local schools were asked to conform to state and federal norms. Local churches, suspect because they were likely not only to express the world view of a particular group or class but also to link it with ultimate values, were accepted only as long as it was understood that they were institutions whose function, like that of the family, was limited to the private sphere of life.

Suburban Religion

In most cases, this conditional acceptance was not experienced by the churches as outside pressure. They felt it appropriate to give up the task of helping to maintain a framework of meaning and identity for the separate cultural groups and became caught up in the new mass culture, in what Gibson Winter has called their "suburban captivity."[6] The postwar period was a time of massive expansion of churches, so much so that main-line denominations often parceled out particular subdivisions to one another so that no one denomination would be overextended and no suburb would be "unchurched." People by and large attended the nearest church of the major faith or broad tradition of their past. Will Herberg saw this as a peculiar process of immigrants as they moved from the ethnic church of the first generation through a secular breakaway of the second generation to a third generation's return to the major faith of their heritage.[7]

But it was a broader movement than that, a kind of "massification" of most denominations, where suburbanized Americans sought religious roots for their new life-styles. They came seeking the kind of community and identity that they had known in their former churches, but one broad enough to encompass the variety of people with whom they now shared their lives. It was important that the teaching, preaching, and programs not express too specifically the uniqueness of each denomination, or the fragile fabric of the religious community might be ripped. It was safer to offer a wide range of activities for people to *do* rather than to deal with hard questions of theology and ethics. The suburban church was a busy place, if not a particularly profound one.

There were some theologians who sought to articulate a vision of a common central faith around which people could form a genuine—and genuinely diverse—community. But these "neo-orthodox" thinkers generally spoke and wrote in styles so intellectual as to have little relation to the busy and shallow life-style of a society shaped by the fictions of popular mass media. Churches that tried to form programs around disciplined teaching of the faith within the family found that only a small core of their members were willing to make that sort of commitment.[8] If in earlier church congregations the regular worship was a celebration of a common life already experienced, in these new ones it was a ritual by which people sought a common experience to express. The coffeepot in the hall was probably a more potent symbol of religious community than the Communion table or altar in the sanctuary. No theological quibbling or liturgical style must endanger that sense of community. Rather, tradition must be adapted to express those facets of life-style which were the only sure commonality of the people in attendance.

Yet the search for primary ties in the suburban congregation was often frustrated by the continuing mobility of members. Many people were moved around the country by organizations they worked for, as these combined and grew and became not local industries but national and multinational corporations. Even those who did not change areas of settlement often changed neighborhoods. As families grew older and larger and their breadwinners ascended the occupational ladder, they moved out of the original subdivision and into larger and more expensive homes. Home ownership was no longer viewed as a permanent investment in a settled neighborhood, but rather as the most available avenue into desired single-family residential neighborhoods. New owners took over old mortgages, and the lending industry developed ways to make it as easy, and as economical, to buy as to rent. But buying did bring with it a greater sense of belonging to the neighborhood. So as people moved, they also moved associational memberships, including those in the church. Their choice of a new church to join often reflected in casual form the sense of ecumenical unity main-line Protestantism was striving for organizationally, accepting without question the assumption of similarity which underlay the comity agreements that had distributed congregations through the suburbs. Depending on the neighborhood, a family might move from Methodist to Congregational to Presbyterian congregations, their way paved by easy acceptance of letters of transfer among most main-line denominations. At the very least, there was massive switching from congregation to congregation, even if denominational loyalty prevailed.

Church programs, then, had to be based much less on the unique talents or experiences of a particular set of members and much more on systematic activities where individuals could be moved in or out without seriously disrupting things. Church programs became almost exoskeletal—boxes into which people could be dropped, activities ready-shaped into which people could fit—rather than outward extensions of the lived commitments of a community of believers. It is probable that never in the history of the Christian church has association with the church been so clearly voluntary. And even the ethnic base of Judaism failed to halt a similar pattern of suburban involvement. People may have come to church or synagogue seeking a true sense of identity in community, but they also approached any particular congregation with the attitude of a consumer. If they did not like the program or the people here, they could go elsewhere.

The Children of the Suburbs

A primary focus of religious programming, as indeed of most of the suburban life of the period, was upon the children. The suburbs were filled with children. Postwar families were much larger than those in Depression years or even in the more prosperous twenties, especially among the middle classes who constituted most of the suburban population, and among the Protestants who were in the main-line churches. It was for the children that adults were involved in most of their voluntary associations—school groups, band or athletic boosters, churches. The children were to be the inheritors of the world for which their parents had suffered the dislocation of the war years and those that followed. The future was something new, untried, experimental, which would be handed over to the young for its culmination.

Schools were the avenue to the future, and parents became passionately involved in advocacy for excellence in education. New psychological findings about the importance of the early years led to great emphasis on kindergarten and nursery school programs. These findings also created considerable tension among parents who distrusted their ability to provide adequate training in this new age for their children. The popularity of books and articles on child rearing grew at a phenomenal rate. Discussion groups and study groups designed to seek and share information on child care proliferated. In a technological age, children came to be seen as the primary product of the family, and status rose and fell with the ability of those children to meet community expectations. All children were expected to be talented; to deserve special lessons in music, art, or dance; to be good athletes; to look good; to use gracefully all the goods and services provided by an indulgent society. The ideal was to be "well-rounded," to take all the talents and products available and weld them into a personal package of responses to the world that would carry one successfully into all the wide-ranging associations of a highly mobile society.

Such high expectations of the young were bound to invoke anxiety not only in their ranks but also among those responsible for their training, anxiety that was not only concerned about the final product of the child-rearing venture but also with the technical expertise with which it was conducted. New levels of education and mass communication had acquainted this generation of parents with at least some of the ideas of Freudian psychology. If nothing else, they were aware that undue repression of basic drives could have serious repercussions. So while they were enjoined to continual efforts to shape children into a mold that was often uncomfortably unfamiliar, they were also cautioned against the use of disciplinary techniques that would be most likely to provide quick and clear evidence that their efforts were effective. Anxious for their children to do well, parents were also awed by the possibility that they might damage their children's egos if they were too demanding. Direct punishment seemed too dangerous a way to induce proper responses. Instead, parents who constantly hovered on the edge of guilt about methods of child rearing learned to control their children with the use of guilt, holding before them the high expectations they were failing to fulfill rather than forbidding behavior that led to their failure to meet the mark.

The positive-thinking theologies of suburban congregations did not have room for discussion of such negative concepts as sin. Rather, the sociological and psychological views by which they were informed tended to treat all negative actions as responses to flaws in the social environment. Parents were not given the old Calvinistic solace of a belief in natural human sinfulness to be expected of a child, out of which he or she could be trained with divine assistance if at all. Rather, the child was seen as a *tabula rasa* upon which the follies of parents might be indelibly etched. No wonder that classes in child rearing became the most successful program item in many congregations! At least the sharing of common experiences and problems offered some relief from the sense of fear and guilt that many parents found endemic to their situation.

One of the failures of these congregations in providing true community involved the loss of contact between generations. Discussion groups in child rearing usually only involved parents who were actively engaged in that task. The older, grandparental generation was frequently underrepresented in the new suburbs. Couples who had moved far from home not only physically, but also psychologically and socially, were not inclined to trust their parents' advice about the rearing of their grandchildren. They seldom considered the possibility that others in that older age group had any more to offer. The future was new; an older generation could not provide guidelines for it. Indeed, activities in most congregations were heavily age-graded. There were few opportunities for people to see what one age group could contribute to another. The nuclear family remained the focus. Church congregations did not provide mediation between them and the larger community; they only provided services and solace for those basic units. And those who were in parts of the family life cycle that did not include children in the home were served separately, in specialized ways, if at all. The notion of a sacred community all "knit and bound together" was seldom raised, much less realized.

The churches, of course, were only part of a much broader cultural pattern. If anything, they were far more inclusive, far less specialized, much deeper in their view of life than other institutions in which most people were involved. In most of the society it seemed that all direction for life was external and impersonal. The company moved families at will; the schools provided their own specialized input into the children's training; the government—more and more at a national rather than a local level—provided legal definitions of responsible public life and ethics. The task for most people was to respond to external stimuli. The adjective of highest commendation was "well-adjusted." Other-directedness, responsiveness to environment, the ability to follow cues to accepted behavior—all seemed to constitute the American way of life.

And in many ways, usually without being aware of it, the churches legitimated, blessed, and taught this approach to the world as an appropriate Christian response. They themselves were large organizations; and parish ministers who were most succcessful were themselves organization men, fully able to relate to the style of life of the mobile suburbs.

It is hardly surprising under these circumstances that many of the children growing up during this period should have experienced the style of life as artificial. Urban living had already accomplished for most people a spatial separation of home from daily work. Suburban living intensified that separation. Not only was the spatial gap much greater as commuting distances grew, but there was also a psychic gap, as settlement patterns tended to scatter broadly the people who worked in any one organization or at any one trade. "Shop talk" was not only found to be dull in the home environment but also potentially divisive, since it would be talk of many diverse "shops" and dissimilar experiences. It was not only impossible for the children to observe their parents at work outside the home, but also it was even hard to listen in on adult conversations about work and those other activities that have traditionally been the most important indicators of persons' place in and contribution to the society. Adult conversations heard by these children tended to center on problems of suburban living—taxes, clubs, crabgrass, and the like—or on the children themselves. Children's experience of most adults was in their role as parents or at recreational activities; so that as these children grew up, their idea of the adult world could easily be one of shallowness and conformity.

There were few experiential bridges other than the recreational ones that led from the world of school and youthful activities to the realities of that wider world inhabited by older generations for which they were supposed to be training. The behavior that children were being taught was not always rooted in observations of adult life. Norms and values seemed to be external, attempts to live up to criteria imposed by outside forces, rather than expressions of a deeply rooted way of life. Advice from the adult world lacked authority in the suburbs.

On the other hand, those young people who lived in traditional towns and neighborhoods were not left untouched by the process. Here adult authority was undermined by the view of the world children were absorbing from the media and which was more and more taught in the schools. The kind of middle-class suburban life constantly portrayed on TV, in movies, books, and magazines became the norm by which most young people understood themselves and their lives, regardless of the positive or negative assessment they might give to such norms. Schools, constrained by national and state requirements, using standardized texts, reinforced a definition of American life not clearly visible in the small-town or rural surroundings of these students. If students were not now of the suburban middle classes, it was assumed that their education should fit them to participate in them as adults.

For many, the image came to seem monolithic, demanding conformity without depth, alienating. But the realization of this and the full alienation that acccompanied this realization did not occur at once. The potential for it developed through their education and for most was confirmed in their experience of the Vietnam war.

Chapter 2

Education for a Dislocated Generation

The period after World War II was often characterized as "child centered." Indeed, it did appear to bring to a peak a characteristic emphasis in American society. A nation consciously attempting to create something better than any of the traditions its people had left behind in their migration to the continent, America has always tended to be oriented toward the future. Children are bearers of the future, and so have been invested with particular importance in this society. In addition, during the early days of the nation, children were important to the regular maintenance of the society simply because there were not enough adults to take all public roles. Thus many young people were thrust early into positions of public responsibility. Voluntary associations for the young, as well as those of the mature, were sources of needed community action; and drives and campaigns of Boy Scouts, Girls Scouts, 4-H Clubs, and a host of others—including church youth groups and Sunday school classes—have provided many important community services.[1]

Thus it was not unusual that the burgeoning suburbs of post-World War II America should emphasize the younger generation. The internal migrations that settled them still bore the marks of future-orientation, the desire to create a life more fulfilling than either the small-town existence of parents' childhood or the crowded temporariness of the war years. The children should be able to grow up participating in the good life of a great nation now risen to world leadership, enjoying a satisfying and cosmopolitan style of life, a life that parents themselves had not experienced or been trained to live.

Postwar Changes in the Schools

Clearly the parents needed help in preparing their children to appropriate the future, the kind of help that had traditionally been provided mobile groups by the educational system. Suburbs were sought out for settlement often on the reputation of their schools or out of the hope that in new communities parents might have some influence on the development of new and better school systems. New buildings, necessitated by the increasing numbers of school children, were expected to have all the latest equipment for teaching, and qualifications for teachers were raised in an attempt to ensure quality.

Then in 1957 an event occurred which was to have profound effect upon the entire educational system. Already perceived as our prime competitors for world leadership, the Russians demonstrated technological superiority by launching into orbit the first space vehicle, Sputnik I. American outcry was instantaneous: How could this have happened? Where was our vaunted American "know-how"? Clearly, we were failing to keep ahead in science and technology at a time when it was crucial to our very existence that we do so. Our world leadership was based largely on our development of the atomic bomb. Cold war perceptions of the world of the Atomic Age were based on knowledge of the tremendous destructive power of modern technology. We dared not let the Russians get ahead of us in this field, for they were the enemy most likely to turn that technology against us. They were pouring apparently unlimited government funds into the development of advanced science and technology and into the training of scientists in their schools and universities. Dare we do otherwise?

So Americans again turned to their educational institutions, this time not only in concern for the quality of life for their children but also with regard to research and training in higher levels of education. The vision became that of a vast research enterprise with people at the top pushing back the frontiers of knowledge with full dedication and support, while lower levels built a solid ladder of training for new generations of scientists. Through the National Science Foundation as well as numerous other channels, the government began pouring funds into those universities capable of supporting major scientific enterprises, and institutions of higher education began to scramble to hire the people and support the programs that could obtain government grants. Grant monies built laboratories, paid salaries of people who worked and taught in them, and provided graduate assistance money for able students to obtain further training. Founded in 1945, the National Science Foundation grew during the 1950s from government appropriations of less than one-fourth million dollars at the beginning of the decade to 136 million dollars at its end. Most of the money went to support basic research, mainly in medical, biological, physical, engineering, and mathematical sciences, and to support scientific manpower, with a large percentage of that category going for graduate fellowships at various levels.

Such support was available not only in the "hard sciences" but also by the end of the decade in those branches of the social sciences that appeared relevant to the situation. Political science gained in importance during the cold war years. Revelations of Chinese Communist success at "brainwashing" American prisoners of war during the Korean conflict gave political importance to the behavioral sciences and enriched the coffers of the National Institute of Mental Health to make it a granting agency to rival the National Science Foundation. Teaching institutions were given particular support for developing new and better ways of teaching science, math, and related subjects through all levels of the school system, and the new emphases were soon reflected in the curricula of all the schools.

Much of this emphasis coming from within the educational system met the hopes and desires of parents, for it was assumed that the future of their children would be based on new science and technology, and it demanded that the nation maintain its domination in international affairs. But the net result was to take most of the direction of the schools out of the hands of local communities and to lodge it instead in distant universities and government agencies. No longer was the primary focus of schooling, even at the primary and secondary levels, that of preparing young people for constructive participation in the local community. Rather, it became clear that real success in school demanded higher education culminating in a research degree; and those who did not reach that lofty goal were to some extent treated as failures, regardless of the patent need of all communities for plumbers, service people, clerks, artisans, and a host of other occupations for which advanced degrees were unnecessary and which might be much more suited to the interests and talents of the students.

"Componential" Education

Meantime, for all the investment in new buildings, new curricula, and better-trained teachers, schools continued to suffer from overcrowding, understaffing, and a shortage of resources. Educational theory stressed the importance of individual attention and allowing children to learn at their own speed, and parents had read enough of the theory to have led their children to expect that kind of education. Yet teachers, faced with overcrowded classrooms, sometimes with double shifts in "split session" days, could not provide genuinely individual attention. Caught between demands for high levels of competency and individual progress, they tended to move toward a more standardized form of teaching. The new educational technologies included "teaching machines," based on giving students immediate feedback as they learned information in small increments, each to be mastered before going on to the next. Even without machines, this method of "programmed learning" became popular. Evaluation of progress was based almost entirely on mastery of small increments of knowledge, or at least such bits of information that could be translated into objective tests where the checking off of a specific choice allowed quick and simple procedures of grading papers for the overworked teacher. Monitoring this process, standing at the gates of higher levels of learning, were standardized tests of a similar type, capable of being graded by computer. These standardized tests were often taken as a measure of the competency not only of the individual students but also of the teacher, the school, and the local system. Education thus came to be equated with the accumulation of specific facts that might or might not be related to any perception of a whole into which they fit in some kind of meaningful relationship.

The division of learning into small components reflected an aspect of the more general process of modernization going on in the world at large. Technological production, argue such observers as Peter Berger[2] and Jacques Ellul,[3] requires that life attain features of "componentiality," where various aspects of a person's life are experienced separately, with little relation to one another. Work is separated from the home; a person's "presentation of self" in those two areas and in various voluntary organizations or other activities in which he or she may be engaged may vary widely. Thus an education that stresses components is in keeping with what is likely to be the life experience of anyone in a modern culture. Trying to pull everything together into a coherent picture can create expectations of a wholeness that is seldom realized in modern life; yet componentiality as a total world view creates problems for a person's sense of identity. When one's life is divided into segments that seem to have little relation to one another, it becomes possible that one not only behaves but also feels like a different person in each of those segments. In that case, it is difficult to attain or maintain a sense of personal identity that remains constant. One's sense of integrity appears compromised under such conditions. It can be maintained only by dissociating the self from the social context in which it is embedded.

The Schools and Alienation

It is evident that education in the expectation of social mobility may appropriately stress the separateness of the individual rather than some visions of a seamless social whole. For many of these young people a componential view of the materials of education did reinforce the way in which they came to perceive themselves—as isolated individuals who might or might not fit into any kind of meaningful social whole. Overcrowded school systems tended to assign them to classes or schools on the basis of impersonal factors or test scores, without consideration of patterns of friendship or outside interests. Always there was held out the expectation that the regimentation at lower levels would be replaced with greater freedom of choice and personal recognition at higher levels of the educational system; so that at least at that time the now unclear features of the individual self might be recognized.

Those whose interests and test scores led them to know that they would not make it into the higher levels frequently became alienated from the whole process, leaving school as soon as the law allowed or some basic level, such as high school graduation, had been reached. Often they left with enough bitterness that it would be difficult for the school to obtain their adult support in later years, and with enough of a sense of separation from fellow students who remained within the system that they would not find any sympathy or understanding for them when later rebellions occurred on college campuses. Though these young people were now assuming responsible social roles, they remained branded educational failures for not going on to higher levels. "Drop-out" became a dirty word, and the person who dropped out felt like an incomplete or flawed human being.

The systemization and impersonalization of the schools varied widely from the rhetoric of child rearing during that period. In fact, conventional wisdom of the time had quite thoroughly discredited earlier emphases on rigid scheduling and discipline from infancy on in favor of a view of the child as innately capable of learning appropriate biological and social responses if allowed to develop without constraint. As we have noted above, this generation of parents had been exposed to modern psychology in college or through the many guidebooks they used in their effort to deal with parenthood in a culture with which they were not familiar enough to be comfortable. They understood, at least at a shallow level, Freudian strictures against repression of basic drives. Parenthood was particularly hard for these new migrants, caught as they were between the poles of anxiety lest they create lasting scars on the psyches of their children and concern lest they not meet the standards of the culture in which they were now participants. All too often they managed to teach children the value of unfettered personal development, while providing blocks to its realization. They rejected the systematic discipline most of their own parents had enforced, frequently substituting for it a kind of *laissez-faire* attitude toward their children until some particular activity or incident triggered concerned reaction. It was almost inevitable that their children should come to find such reactions both severe and arbitrary. By the time the children reached adolescence, many had come to distrust their parents' judgment and concern for them. It is not surprising that they should transfer that distrust to their teachers, particularly under the circumstances of their schooling.

Even if parents had provided model environments for their development, schools in this setting could not provide these environments, at least for most of their students. Regimented, impersonal schooling was frustrating, and frustration was defined as a serious problem rather than the source of challenge it might have been considered in an earlier time. High school students read college catalogs that proclaimed humanitarian values for their institutions, pointing out their many resources for personal growth and development; and students assumed that the frustrations they had felt in secondary school would be compensated with freedom and personalism in higher education. Those who did not go on to college felt cheated of the chance for such an experience. But those who went to college found again the overcrowded classrooms, standardized tests, computer-assigned programs, and overworked teaching staff that had alienated them in high school. They had lived through months and years of hard work and anxiety in order to get into the best colleges and study under the best professors, only to find themselves in huge classes taught by graduate students who clearly found their greatest rewards not in teaching but in the hours that they could spend in the laboratory or seminar with the great professor. The message was clear: The purpose of education was to become one of that small coterie of advanced students, to do research. All else was secondary. The true center of the educational system seemed to be the scientific laboratory. This tended to be most true at the colleges with the highest reputations; so that it is no wonder that when rebellion broke out, it tended to be centered on those campuses.

In the experience of students, and in the actual structure of the society, education became a separate, almost isolated institution, pursuing its own goals and values with little consideration for other institutions or needs of the society. Even in acceding to government pressure for scientific information, researchers often wrote proposals that seemingly met the aims of purveyors of grants but could be used primarily to pursue personal scientific interests at some distance from the topics of public concern. It was assumed that the scientists could better gauge the importance of their endeavors than those who merely paid the bills. Those furthest in pursuit of the goals of scientific excellence became something of a law unto themselves. And the reward system at all levels of the educational system was governed mostly by the values at the top, often stressing arcane knowledge above immediately useful skills by which society or self might be served. If indeed the research was oriented to practical needs, it seemed always to be the needs of the rich and the powerful, not those of the majority of the society or of the students themselves. The entire endeavor seemed to have lost all human qualities.

The attitudes of scientific research dominated the university. Its most important focus was on the art of critical thinking—on the ability to disengage oneself from the object of study enough to look at it without prejudice, analyzing its merits and its faults, its uses and dangers, by some set of criteria external to it. This is relatively easy to do when the object of study is a star, an atom, a machine, or even a frog. There seemed little reason to question the appropriateness of that approach in the study of the "hard sciences," at least at the time. However, there are different consequences when that kind of critical analysis is turned on one's own species and one's culture. The biological sciences tended to treat humankind as only one of the vast array of living organisms on this planet. They offered little basis for the sense of special destiny that has inspired the creation and maintenance of human culture. Similarly, psychology's uncovering of unconscious drives that can impel people to particular behavior often led to a loss of self-esteem on the part of individual students still unsure of their own identity. The social sciences, in their consideration of social and cultural forms as consequences of group survival needs and class interest, gave little basis for cultural or group loyalty. The critical-objective influence in the humanities emphasized the relative nature of human culture rather than any sense of moral absolutes; it tended to define loyalty to particular cultural expressions as narrow chauvinism.

At high levels of education, where frontiers of knowledge and culture are being transcended, disengagement from conventional wisdom and narrow identification is both useful and appropriate. But as the educational system was upgraded by demanding that teachers obtain higher degrees and those higher degrees were dominated by research-oriented objective values, critical-analytical thinking came to be the goal of education at all levels. Younger and younger students were taught to view themselves, other people, and their social and cultural surroundings, as well as other species, the earth, and the universe, from a position of critical detachment. No longer was history taught as the story of a society into which the young were being initiated. Rather, historians demanded of the young that they hold themselves critically aloof from the society whose patterns they had not yet mastered. Literature was seldom taught as the expression of basic themes and values of the society, the sharing of which could bring them into full participation with one another within the culture. Frequently it was not even presented in ways that could stimulate aesthetic enjoyment but rather from a critical standpoint: What were the forms the artist was trying to follow? What psychological or sociological quirks were being expressed in the work? Expressions of value or loyalty were often treated as efforts to manipulate people's response, to restrict their freedom to be detached and critical. In such settings, work without form, work with no message, tended to be rated highest, as most honest.

The demand for critical detachment had more sources than the scientific method, sources more consistent with the liberal arts tradition. The society had just emerged from a war whose primary cause was believed to have been the ability of dictatorial governments to promote in their people a level of fanaticism that denied human rights and free thought. The primary understanding of the cold war of the 1950s was that communism was a similar totalitarian philosophy, to be resisted in the name of individual freedom. The definition of democracy came to be seen almost exclusively as the freedom of the individual to resist any demands of the society or the culture. Anything that benefited the group was treated as inimical to the good of the individual. Only the person who transcended all group loyalties could be fully free and fully human.

The anomaly of such an ideology imbedded in a society whose primary character was the "organization man" was all too clear. Neither did it help that it was taught in a school system more and more bureaucratically organized, less and less able to provide individualized instruction for its teeming population. Students were inclined to perceive the tension as one more evidence of the hypocrisy of adult society.

Schools became the target of mounting ambivalence, attracting loyalty as the one institution focused upon students and their needs, yet providing in their very values the basis of alienation from education as well as other social institutions. Children and young people tended to have their lives dominated by the schools. It was in the school that they found most of their friends and formed most of their loyalties. As work became more and more separated from the home, it was primarily in the school that young people were able to see adults at work. Fathers and mothers might work in distant offices, factories, or stores; teachers and professors were available for observation and imitation. They became the most important adult role models. Since they were engaged in the production of new knowledge, they seemed more reliable than parents or other adults as sources of interpretation of events and values. The school might seem oppressive and frustrating, but it was the only institution in which young people felt they played a part. Yet it seemed very separate from the rest of the society; it no longer appeared consciously to be training them for competency to participate in other institutions.

Emphases on science and math tended to demonstrate incompetence in parents since much of the content of their children's texts had been developed in recent years, and such approaches as the "new math" were cast in language unfamiliar to most of the older generation. Social studies, in like manner, had changed, taking an objective if not a debunking view toward all the verities of history and culture taught in earlier times. Students were shown the weaknesses of the political and economic systems in which they were reared, and they learned to be critics of all taken-for-granted assumptions.

For many young people experience reinforced attitudes of disengagement from social institutions. In a quickly urbanizing society with massive population growth, few communities had the place for responsible public involvement of the young that had been the custom in underpopulated small towns. Child labor and minimum wage laws, union shops, and increased specialization all narrowed the chances of young people to be gainfully employed and so incorporated into the economic structure of the society. Even home chores that contributed to the economic welfare of the family shrank to near meaninglessness with new technology in the home. Far from needing assistance with their work, parents whose occupations were distant from the home often had more leisure time than they had learned to use constructively. When they did find constructive outlets, these often took over the public functions of many of the voluntary associations of the young, thus again reducing meaningful participation in the life of the wider community for young people. Adult service organizations took over some of the community betterment projects once handled by youth organizations and often even did the fund raising for the latter groups. In their activities, young people were related to the community as passive clients rather than as active participants. It became apparent to many students that one important societal function of the schools was to keep them out of an overcrowded labor marketplace and community action, no matter what they felt they might contribute. It was hard to continue to see the school in a positive light from such a point of view.

Young people turned their critical gaze toward the attempts at cultural construction so common to many of their parents and found them flawed. Mass-produced culture, dictated by commercial purveyors of the good life through the mass media, was labeled "plastic." A favorite popular song characterized suburban living as "little boxes on the hillside, little boxes made of ticky tacky."[4] The shallowness of relationships, the exterior forms of conformity and value, were excoriated by tastemakers in education, a value accepted by students for whom they were the cultural arbitors. Only by remaining separate could they avoid contamination from the sick shallowness and mediocrity of the society. As a consequence, young people came to devalue any expressive activities that related them to institutions, whether in their families, among their peers, or in their schools and clubs. The "rituals of intensification" that had bound young people to social institutions in this and all cultures were questioned. Ball games, pep rallies, proms, and the like came to be shunned as manipulative occasions engineered to develop a loyalty that could reduce their freedom and individuality. Family gatherings, religious rituals, and other expressive institutional activities were similarly held suspect.

Dealing with the War

Their disaffection and withdrawal from institutional involvement could have been passed off as short-lived forms of youthful rebellion with small lasting import if this generation of young people had not been provided evidence of the alienage and enmity of the society outside the educational institution. Sacrificing personal development for success in school or occupation was one thing. It was something else to sacrifice one's life in order to save the face of a society with which one had little sense of identity. And that is how the Vietnam war came to be perceived by many students, an evaluation shared, if not taught, by many of their instructors. Many academics had been involved directly or indirectly in civil rights activism, and for some this had included acts of civil disobedience. There was little doubt on campus that citizens had the right and duty to criticize their government, even to take action against it when they felt it to be in the wrong. Much of the political science and social psychological research of the period dealt with the problem of sources of Nazism in prewar Germany. In the social sciences and the literature there were many allusions to the danger of obedience to a corrupt state. Even chemists and physicists were concerned with the danger of allowing the products of their research to become political tools, given the horror of atomic warfare. Critical analyses of past wars had revealed the manipulative uses of patriotism and the nature and uses of propaganda. Thus the universities were ready to pass judgment on a government bent on pursuing a scarcely justifiable war while their students dealt with it as a personal threat.

At first, students were deferred from the draft until they finished their academic programs. To continue that deferment, many went into graduate programs in which they might otherwise have had little interest. Professors, faced with the knowledge that a failing grade or poor recommendation for further study might have the effect of a death sentence by making a student eligible for immediate drafting, chose not to give failing marks. Particularly in classes too large for personal contact between professor and student, they had considerable doubt about the accuracy of their evaluations, at least when weighed in a balance of life and death. It was from that time that many professors began to agitate for nongraded courses, making the relativism which they taught the guide for their teaching methods. They refused to make judgments. Once begun, this practice did not recede when student deferments were no longer available.

At this time, when students were in immediate jeopardy of the draft, many teachers and counselors on college campuses offered assistance to students seeking conscientious-objector status, and in some cases they even helped set up underground railways that allowed young men to escape the country rather than serve in the war. Here the separation of the educational institution from that of government became very real.

This separation was never total, of course. People in those programs and in many colleges that were aimed at more immediately practical learning that would indeed tie students into specific places in the social and institutional structure outside the university, or who still held to the assumption that education is primarily initiation into society and culture, tended to resist the rebellion at their doorsteps. But in many cases their protests were unheard, and the colleges became the setting for more and more vigorous protest against the war. The adversary relationship between government and the colleges was not just one-sided, as became evident when the release of the infamous White House tapes demonstrated the attitude of the Nixon administration toward students and those adults who aided them.

The Formation of a Counterculture

But the alienation of the young was not just from the government. They had come to view the entire society as inimical to their interests, finding the schools being used to shape them to the needs of a society and an economy they felt no call to serve, pushing them into actions and goals alien to their own desires and talents for the purposes of an alien "system." The cry of the war protesters, "Hell, no, I won't go!" was echoed in far broader contexts, and the rebellion turned on the culture at large, seeking to create a new and more satisfying way of living in the world.

The breadth of the counterculture that arose gives evidence of the amount of alienation felt by this group of young people. Accusing the society of having alienated them from themselves, they sought to recover a romanticism lost in the pragmatic world view of technical science. They sought new levels of experience, often with the help of hallucinogenic drugs they claimed to be mind-expanding. Alienated from their families, they sought new forms of close association, from casual coupling to intense communities. Alienated from the economy, they refused to prepare themselves for work ordinarily deemed successful and resorted instead to a barter economy and a subsistence existence, sharing what they had, hitchhiking from place to place, begging, working at odd jobs. Alienated from the schools, they set up free universities, where people could share knowledge with one another without tuition and without grades or credentials. Alienated from the churches and synagogues, they invented new religions or tried to reconstitute ancient ones, seeking mystery, community, and celebration in ways far removed from the friendly "busyness" of the suburban congregations out of which many of them had come.

The percentage of those who became fully immersed in the counterculture was relatively small, but various phases of it touched a broad segment of this age group in particular and the society at large as well. One of the primary agencies of contact was music. The counterculture developed an even more distinctive style from the rock 'n' roll of the fifties. Their protest was in the words of many of the songs, but perhaps even more in the primitive rhythms and overwhelming amplification of sound. Their music was indeed a protest against the secular rationality of their upbringing; no rational conversation could be carried on within range of the music. Accompanied by throbbing light shows and often by drug use as well, the music of the counterculture was total experience. It provided its own communal rituals, its own isolation from those unable or unwilling to penetrate the sound barrier.

Performers of the music also gave leadership in style of dress and grooming that set the counterculture apart and were themselves symbols of protest. A generation raised in the gleaming new homes of suburbia, watching all the laundry ads on television, made dirt a symbol of freedom. Young men whose childhood had featured short-clipped postwar hairstyles now eschewed scissors and razors entirely. If there was any one item of personal grooming that most symbolized the counterculture, it was hair—long and free-flowing on men and women, beards untrimmed, curlers and hairdressers foregone, hair in wild abandon. It is not a coincidence that one of the most popular celebrations of the counterculture was the musical *Hair*.

At its inception, there was a passionate vigor about the counterculture, a sense of creativity and freshness that made it very attractive. It became, undeniably, a media event. Variety shows featured countercultural musicians; talk shows interviewed protest leaders, musicians, all types of cultural experimenters. At a time when the experience of many young people was isolation from the mainstream of the society, these countercultural celebrities made youth the focus of public attention, gave them a sense of importance and value. Young people who would never become full participants in the counterculture still sought to emulate these youthful celebrities. They aped their style of dress, let their hair grow long, and often found themselves treated like public enemies because their appearance was indistinguishable from that of dedicated revolutionaries. In many cases, a vicious circle developed in which expressions of minor alienation were met by anger and repression, thus generating greater levels of alienation. High schools were torn by controversy over dress codes and grooming regulations as adults sought to regulate the teaching environment and students claimed violations of their civil rights.

But not all adults were offended by the counterculture. A significant number, many in educational institutions, looked to the counterculture as a genuine social experiment which could provide new patterns for a society that seemed to be losing its direction and cohesion. Perhaps the most eloquent adult advocate of the counterculture was the man who popularized the term, Theodore Roszak, a humanities professor at a state university in California. His book, *The Making of a Counterculture*,[5] became a best seller and provided a basic statement of an ideology for the movement. He made a convincing case for the bankruptcy of the culture against which this new rebellion had come that seemed to fit Yeats's ominous vision in "The Second Coming":

> Turning and turning in the widening gyre
> The falcon cannot hear the falconer;
> Things fall apart; the centre cannot hold;
> Mere anarchy is loosed upon the world,
> The blood-dimmed tide is loosed, and everywhere
> The ceremony of innocence is drowned;
> The best lack all conviction, while the worst
> Are full of passionate intensity.
>
> Surely some revelation is at hand;
> Surely the Second Coming is at hand.
> The Second Coming! Hardly are those words out
> When a vast image out of *Spiritus Mundi*
> Troubles my sight: Somewhere in the sands of the desert
> A shape with lion body and the head of a man,
> A gaze blank and pitiless as the sun,
> Is moving its slow thighs, while all about it
> Reel shadows of indignant desert birds.
> The darkness drops again; but now I know
> That twenty centuries of stony sleep
> Were vexed to nightmare by a rocking cradle,
> And what rough beast, its hour come round at last,
> Slouches towards Bethlehem to be born?[6]

This particular "rough beast," he felt, was a justifiable protest against the "single vision" of science, which made no allowance for mystery or expressiveness.

Many serious students of culture and society noted hopeful aspects of the movement. Particularly in intellectual circles, people were highly critical of postwar developments in the culture. It was from them that the young had learned to criticize the shallowness and mass-produced nature of the suburban life-style, and many saw the counterculture as a road to a more attractive alternative. These students of culture and society added to the usual future-orientation of American culture a belief that the speed of change had outdistanced the ability of adults to respond creatively. Margaret Mead, particularly in her *Culture and Commitment,* wrote of parents as aliens in a land so changed that their socialization had in no way prepared them for it. In traditional societies, she wrote, parents could anticipate the lives their children would lead in the future and were adequate guides to that future. As change accelerated, parents and children came to be partners in exploring the nature and potential of the future. But in modern society, it was her contention, only the children had been adequately prepared to deal with the speed of change. Parents must now look to them for guidance.[7]

If only the children could deal with the future, then they would have to develop the culture of a future society. Such thinking clearly implied involvement with the counterculture on the part of educational institutions. The laboratories of the scientists had been expected to provide new knowledge and new skills with which to meet the future. Now the entire campus was envisioned as a laboratory for social and cultural experimentation, undertaken by the young but encouraged by some of their academic mentors. Codes of conduct and the responsibility of colleges to act as surrogate parents must be abrogated so that the experiments could take place free of extraneous influences. The sanctity of the campus must not be breached by police or the military, for even if some of the experimental behavior were illegal or subversive at the moment, it might become normative in the new world of the future. Such attitudes not only increased the isolation of education from other institutions of the society, but they also justified it.

Isolating the university is nothing particularly new. Town-gown squabbles over the activities of students and their relation to the mores of adult society have been endemic at least since the time when Socrates was condemned for leading astray the youth of Athens, and probably long before that. The only distinctive difference in this case is that earlier student rebels were only a small elite of the society, while today nearly all young people seem to be students. While the genuine cultural experimenters probably constituted no larger a percentage of the society than those earlier student troublemakers, emulation of them by other students in matters of dress, grooming, and manners made it impossible for most observers to separate the two groups. *All* students were seen as radical revolutionaries by opponents of the counterculture. On the other hand, the movement's proponents sought to protect *all* student behavior as cultural experimentation, no matter how foolish it might be.

One ironic feature of the situation was that in most cases the real cultural experimentation was not occurring on the campuses. To be fully a part of the counterculture, one could hardly be a student because the counterculture was a protest against all institutions, including the schools. This was evident in some university towns, where conflict between students and "street people" was always threatening. But since students had taken on so many of the trappings of the counterculture, outsiders could see no difference. Their styles made visible a generation gap that grew with the growth of the counterculture. People threatened by the implicit cultural criticism in the behavior of "hippies" tended to lump all youth together into an outcast status. This, in turn, fueled the fires of alienation and increased the width of separation. The slogan of the young became "Don't trust anyone over thirty!"

It is at this point that we must take note of an often-ignored aspect of the youth of this period—the deep and fundamental division within their ranks. While alienation from at least some aspects of the educational system may have been fairly general, the way in which it took form was quite different among those who became disillusioned with higher education and those who had not attained that level of academic endeavor. For the latter, other parts of the society were now providing the identity and sense of worth the schools may have denied them. Many were now filling adult roles in the society, were attached to the economic structure through jobs, were married and attempting to establish traditional families. Their position at the beginning of more or less traditional careers made them, perhaps, somewhat less confident of themselves than their older co-workers. The anti-institutional behavior of countercultural young people was often a particular threat to them. So when confrontations arose between young demonstrators and "hard hats," many of the most adamant of the latter were in that supposedly magical age category of "under thirty." By far the most tragic incident that pitted these two groups of young people against one another was the shooting of four student protesters at Kent State University by National Guardsmen who were, in the main, the same age.

The division could also be found on campuses. In a 1968 survey of college students by the Yankelovich organization significant differences were found between those defined as "career-minded" and "post-affluent." The latter, of course, were oriented toward the counterculture, if not fully within it, and constituted some 44 percent of the sample. The study showed more than twenty percentage points' difference between the two groups on such issues as the sacredness of private property, emphases on law and order, and their evaluation of the functions of competition. Post-affluent students were far less supportive of parental authority within the family, and indeed of any kinds of authority, and were much less appreciative of the value of hard work than the career-minded. They were much more supportive of sexual freedom and experimentation in living arrangements and more willing to express dissatisfaction with the political processes of the country and to support radical action to institute change.[8]

The influence of the post-affluent was probably greater than their actual proportion, given their high visibility. Not only did they stand out because of their dress and style of life, but they also made good journalistic copy; they were "news." Evidence of their influence can be found in a second survey made by the Yankelovich group in 1973. This showed a lessening of the gap between the groups, as selected countercultural values were sifting into the blue-collar ranks, and the harshness of cultural criticism was becoming somewhat more muted among the post-affluent.[9] However, most of the young people covered in the second survey constituted a younger age cohort. The significance of that difference is something more appropriate for the discussion in chapter 4. Suffice it to say that in the group most affected by the counterculture the division has softened with age, but is retained primarily in the understanding that the postwar years have produced a "new class" of people whose relation to production and to major institutions of the society is different from that of earlier groups that have dominated the society and set its tone.[10] This "new class" is not only the product of the postwar educational system but also has had a significant influence in its recent development. However, that subject is beyond the scope of the present discussion.

Impacting the Society

The way in which the separateness of the counterculture was transmuted into new social forms is worth considering. For many of the youthful rebels the cause of personal freedom was sufficient, and they spent full time creating situations in which they might "do their own thing." Yet there were at least two ways in which they were called out of the essential selfishness of this kind of rebellion—one based on their own need for mutual aid, the other coming out of their conviction that freedom from oppressive institutions was the right of many other groups in the society besides themselves. One of the primary areas of mutual aid was developed out of the drug culture. Experimentation with hallucinogenic drugs led many young people through "bad trips" that were both terrifying and dangerous to mental and physical health. Yet the illegal nature of the drugs prevented their seeking out ordinary sources of help at hospitals and counseling centers. Instead, they turned to one another, helping one another through crises, nursing one another back to health. In many areas the counterculture began to develop alternative institutions, the earliest of which were often free clinics for the treatment of illnesses either held to be illicit in mainstream society or ordinarily requiring expensive treatment of those who had foregone a money economy. In the process of helping one another through crises of genuine seriousness, many young people had their first experience of really being needed by someone else and of being able to meet at least some of those needs. Their rebellion against the instrumental values of much of their training was confirmed in the gentle caring for one another they came to experience in such situations and in the equally illicit activities of protecting young men from the draft.

Activities on behalf of people outside the youth counterculture were often based on experiences or stories of civil rights activism earlier in the decade. Members of the counterculture had found clear evidence of the oppressiveness of "the system" in the systemic racism of American society and so assumed that blacks, and indeed all minority groups, needed to be freed from dominant institutions as they themselves felt the need. Much of the action regarding this issue involved political discussions of a Marxist hue, though often their Marxism was selective. Their actual involvement in the process of political change ranged from working in election campaigns to terrorist attempts to bomb centers of institutional power. Some of these young people even ran for political office, and in a few unique places, such as Berkeley, were able to gain sufficient influence in the city government to pass rent control ordinances and similar actions aimed to benefit both the voluntary poor of the counterculture and those in the community for whom poverty was endemic. Other young people in this movement sought to free the oppressed through acts of personal service. Many acted out of a deep sense of idealism and commitment, others in a random or faddish way.

Familiar as they were with the educational system and its perceived disservice to them, many of these young people went into the public schools as teachers, teachers' aides, or unpaid volunteers in an effort to humanize the educational system. Inspired by such critics of the system as Paul Goodman, John Holt, and Jonathan Kozol, they sought to mitigate the effects of educational bureaucracies in the lives of young students, to find ways of overcoming the effects of poverty and cultural deprivation in the lives of children in the inner city and in rural pockets of poverty.

Often the primary criticism leveled at the schools by the counterculture was that the only values they reflected were those of the consumer society. Young people participating in the educative process attempted to introduce what they believed to be more humanistic values. But they sometimes became entangled in a situation where the subject of values reflected far more than the simple polarities they had perceived. As processes of school integration progressed and criticism of the system became more widespread, the schools found themselves buffeted by demands of many interest groups to have their interests and values represented. Bilingual education; realistic portrayal of minorities; equal treatment of females in textbooks, classrooms, and on the playing fields; and questions of interpretation of history—all clouded the perception of school officials as to the task of education. Were children to be trained to one model of American citizenship, or many? How could each student or student group be affirmed in its particularity and yet be taught to improve? What, indeed, was improvement? Teachers, be they traditional or countercultural, began to find it impossible to work with models of education by which they had previously framed their goals. In the meantime, with classrooms now filled with students of highly diverse backgrounds that made it difficult to interpret one another's behavior or to respond similarly to teachers' cues, much of the activity of the schools became a mere attempt to maintain order. Without a shared value system in which to locate their authority, teachers often failed even in that minimal task.

One of the alternative institutions born of the counterculture was the "alternative school," in which their version of humanistic values could be expressed not just by individuals trying to cope with the educational system but by the entire system. The rigid pattern of age-grading children and structuring school days into a number of periods of equal length was abandoned in favor of open classrooms in which older youngsters might help younger ones and the entire group go on field trips or enjoy special activities. Dress codes were abandoned, language was free, and learning was often a strictly voluntary affair.

In certain cities around the country some of the alternative schools were accepted into the public school system as a choice open to parents who would prefer their children to learn in a more permissive environment. More often, they proved to be experimental centers out of which some teaching methods, in modified form, were transferred to the official system. Alternative schools also served a function unintended by their counterculture creators. Their presence in the society encouraged conservative groups to develop their own alternatives that would concentate on the "basics" and provide a highly structured, disciplined environment for their students.

Other alternative schools developed in reaction to perceptions of oppression in the official system. These included schools begun by the Black Panthers, intended to instill in black children racial pride as well as political consciousness, and others coming out of Marxist or other political movements. In highly pluralistic urban areas, the variety of schools offered some kind of solution to the faltering classroom that was trying to be all things to all people but at the cost of direct experience of cultural pluralism by the children. In areas more dominated by traditional values the alternative was often a church-sponsored "Christian school," where conservative Christian values could be taught without apology and firm discipline could be exercised in the name of ascetic values and a common model of the ideal person. In some parts of the country these were "segregation academies," created simply to avoid interracial education. But in other places they were responses less to racism than to cultural pluralism, supported by parents who found the lack of clear models in a pluralistic classroom a threat to their values and their definition of their children's needs.

Most of these developments occurred after the student years of the particular age group most central to this discussion. The changes were rather a response to their activities as students and were, in many cases, initiated by them. In particular, the alternative schools were the product of this age group and evidence of their determination to change an educational system they had found alienating. These schools were expressions of their idealism, evidence of how thoroughly they had accepted the idea that human development was inhibited by social institutions and must instead be freed to reach its inherent potential.

Targeting the Universities

The counterculture's most immediate and recognized effect, however, occurred at higher levels of education. Four issues were raised on campus concerning the uses and program of the university. The first was political, with students demanding the right to participate in structures of university governance that involved decision making concerning their education and campus life. Second was a move against traditional teaching methods and curricula, with a demand for more "relevance" in course content and for reconsideration of traditional grading practices in favor of greater democratization and lessened competition in the classroom. The third, tied to political movements outside the campus that eventually resulted in lowering many aspects of legal adulthood from age twenty-one to age eighteen, concerned college supervision, *in loco parentis*, of the lives of students. Finally, attacks were made on the ways in which colleges limited their availability through testing, academic records, and tuition, with the demand that higher education serve the people not only with the expertise of study and laboratory but also by opening up the classrooms which held the key to entrance into the mainstream of American economic and social life.

In each case, the universities moved toward meeting the demands of their students and those faculty involved in the student movements, and in each case ripples of change extended beyond the immediate action. Participation in university governance was granted in many schools, with students placed on committees supervising curricular planning, faculty hiring, budgetary concerns, admissions, and other matters previously reserved to faculty or administrators. Some schools even made a place for student members on their governing boards. But the changes expected in the university through such participation never significantly materialized. Students were seldom given a majority voice in decision making. And by the time the changes went into effect, many of the students who had demanded the right to participate had been succeeded by a generation unwilling to devote the necessary time and effort to details of school administration that might have made an impact. In some schools those channels for student participation still exist, serving more often as avenues for a few student leaders to gain influence and executive skill than to change the university.

The demand for curricular revision met with a somewhat similar fate but with more lasting results in a few areas. One element of the demand, though seldom clearly expressed at the beginning, was a more general disaffection with the dominance of the research universities over all the rest of the educational system. For students who first pushed for curricular change during this period, the issue was one of relevance of their studies to their own lives and immediate needs. Too often the work of classroom and laboratory seemed far removed from their experience. Learning was objective, distant, sanitized of human warmth and emotion, impractical in any setting other than school or lab.

An example of the way in which their rebellion was encouraged by some of the very processes it protested could be seen in the field of psychology. On the one hand, students complained about the clinical approach to human personality, the coldness and distance reflected in experiments for which they often served as subjects. On the other hand, this rational, objective science had proved in its experiments that human beings have needs beyond the rational, that for normal personality development one needs to experience the warmth of human contact, outlets for emotional response, avenues for nonrational behavior. Among the scholars who provided a rationale for student rebellion were psychologists who were themselves in conflict with certain forms of their own discipline. Particularly important to this movement was the work of such persons as Abraham Maslow, Carl Rogers, R. D. Laing, Rollo May, and Erich Fromm, and the movement that became known as "humanistic psychology." Out of this movement grew others variously identified as "sensitivity training," "awareness training," and the "human potential movement," among others. The primary educational philosophy fostered by this branch of psychology defined education much more as the stimulation of individuals to become aware of and to develop their own inner resources than as the imparting of facts. Clearly this clashed with the data-oriented ideas of programmed learning, whose psychological base might be found in the behaviorist tradition, personified for many by B. F. Skinner. The lines of conflict may easily be seen by comparing Skinner's *Beyond Freedom and Dignity,* with its understanding of processes of conditioning people to fit societal needs, and the *Journal of Transpersonal Psychology,* begun by Maslow, where the emphasis is on cultivating "peak experiences" and awareness in terms close to those of some religious traditions.

Students affected by the counterculture tended to favor the basic views of humanistic psychology. Their experience of social institutions as inimical to their own needs and desires led them to an understanding of Skinnerian conditioning as an evil plot against the right to individual growth and development. Classrooms, they felt, were fitting them into a society alien to them, shaping them into unwanted forms. Authoritarian patterns of lectures and objective, often machine-graded, tests evaluated on the basis of the statistical normal curve were defined as inhumane, violating basic understandings of true human development. Competition for grades and awards stressed a definition of human nature they sought to deny; they demanded the right of individuals to develop in their own way and at their own speed, cooperating on work, learning by doing. They demanded that schools recognize the value of learning outside the classroom and of the development in ways other than the accumulation of isolated facts.

The primary effect of their demand for noncompetitive education came in the grading systems of many colleges. In many, an option simply to give credit without attaching a grade was opened to teachers, to be used in courses where they considered them appropriate or to be chosen by students who preferred not to enter competition for grades. The latter gave one of many indications of the split between those designated by Yankelovich as "post-affluent" and "career-minded." Career-minded students tended to remain competitive, to seek to retain grading systems that would indicate to future employers the quality of their scholastic work.

The issue of university oversight of the private lives of students had a somewhat different outcome, one that increased the alienation of the young on campus and off. On many campuses it offered a rationale for college administrators to move out of an area where they had been increasingly losing their effectiveness. It also exacerbated a dilemma in the understanding of the nature of the university. One of the most time-honored traditions of the university has been its freedom from control of the society outside its bounds. In order for the pursuit of truth to continue unhampered by political, economic, religious, or other forces in the society, universities have long protected their boundaries, giving professors tenured positions that would let them be free of outside pressure, fighting for freedom from supervision by local police or other agents of social control, demanding control over their own domain. Experimentation with new ideas, says the tradition, should not be restricted. But now students' primary areas of experimentation lay in new life-styles that came in direct conflict with societal standards. Unlike more traditional student "high jinks," the activities taken up by students during this period had an ideological base. They spoke of experimenting in life-styles not as a temporary "fling" but as an attempt at solutions to problems they perceived in the wider society. Several types of experimentation seemed particularly subversive of the "American way." First, in a culture which had historically opposed all hallucinogenic drugs as inevitably addictive and destructive of human will, they insisted upon exploring the inner reaches of their consciousness with the help of such drugs. Second, in violation of generations of acceptance of the work ethic and a definition of human nature as innately competitive, they were attempting communal and cooperative forms of living and relating to economic forces, accepting subsistence levels of income as sufficient. Not only did this violate many of society's basic assumptions, but it also aroused political fears about the relation of communal living to political communism, fears further stimulated by Marxist rhetoric within some groups on campus. A third problematic area of experimentation was often related to the practice of communal living, that of experimenting with sexual relations and alternatives to the traditional family. These ranged from group marriages to casual sexual unions or homosexual liaisons and again were supported by ideological statements of the essential rightness of all such alliances. Growing levels of such experimentation made university supervision of dormitory life difficult, to say the least, and often coincided with student refusal to live in college-owned-and-operated housing. Thus it was often with considerable relief that universities gave in to students' demands that they quit acting *in loco parentis* and confine their concern for students to their classroom performance. University officials, by deciding to move in that direction, freed themselves from responsibility for the actions of students they felt they could no longer control.

One of the consequences of this action was the upsetting of the delicate balance between universities and their surrounding communities. One way in which universities had been able to maintain "free space" for experiments and unpopular opinion was by taking responsibility for maintaining order within that space. Students and faculty alike were protected from incursions of outside forces only by their ability to insulate the rest of the society from consequences of any violation of their norms that occurred on campus. But from the Free Speech Movement in Berkeley to the sometimes violent takeovers of buildings on many campuses, educational institutions found it harder and harder to control actions of their students directed toward their own administrations. And when those students insisted on living off campus in styles that violated building codes, health codes, moral codes, and state and federal laws, school administrations could no longer shelter them from the self-protective actions of local communities. Sometimes administrators deliberately sought aid from National Guard units or other agencies to control students on campus. At other times they simply stood aside as students off campus were subjected to local law enforcement. Many campus officials tried at times to rescue students from severe reactions of the "locals," but it became harder and harder for them to justify doing so. In the long run, students' demands for freedom to experiment in life-styles resulted in a loss of freedom from outside pressure for all elements of the university.

It was also this facet of university rebellion that had the widest consequences in the society at large. News of collegiate rebels led many adults to a greater distrust of all youth, and so they looked to the institution of repressive measures to keep the rebellion from spreading. In particular, high school administrators often reacted defensively when any student criticism of the schools arose, bringing to mind images of violent revolution on campus. Police who had been called to quell riots on campus were more likely to look at all young people as potential criminals and to reevaluate actions once considered youthful pranks as antisocial behavior to be punished. Thus direct proof of the enmity of adult society was once more given to the young.

The final area of activity, that of attempting to open the university to a wider range of applicants, has coincided with other political movements against discrimination and educational development such as the junior college movement. It is hard to say how much of the rebellion of this age cohort really contributed to such developments, or how much its alienation helped to foster some of the disillusionment that has occurred among some of its clients. The desire to spread the benefits of education, if nothing else, indicates the ambivalence of those who were working for such causes at the same time that they were attempting to tear down many of the structures of the educational system. It is also interesting to note that many of the free universities once thought to open opportunity to the poor have now become centers of continuing education for affluent young adults once part of the countercultural generation.

The Dilemma of the Schools

There appear to be several reasons for the focus on educational change during this period. The greater isolation of young people from other social institutions as their lives were dominated by their schools made the schools the only available target for much of their frustration. The sheer size of this particular age cohort gave them social importance. But also, in a larger setting, the targeting of the schools was a natural response to the particular importance given the educational institution during that period. As the "great migration" of the war and postwar years and the technological change of the time tore apart traditional patterns of distributing people through the various occupational and status positions of the society, the school became almost the sole gatekeeper to social and economic advancement. For students who were the children of a generation that found places in a reordered society through higher education funded by the GI Bill and research grants, the pattern was so taken for granted that any movement for social equality or social change was assumed to need to focus on the schools as well as on the government that was expected to support those schools.

However, the various movements of the time laid conflicting burdens on the schools, expectations that could not be met within a single institution. Schools, from elementary to college level, had long served as pathways into the social and economic mainstream for persons in marginal groups—immigrants, the poor, the isolated. They had done so in two ways, by providing basic occupational and social skills, and by teaching the young a common vision of American life and purpose upon which they could build a structure of shared values and goals. The outlines of what has come to be called America's "civil religion" were inculcated in the schools, and upon that base were overlaid the values of the "meritocracy" of higher education. Ideals of excellence were linked to notions of upward striving and mobility on a generally recognized ladder of success, with certain symbols of status—usually found in a family's style of life—understood to indicate relative placement on the ladder. Individual advancement on that ladder was equated with social good in the understanding that personal advancement was a reward for contributions to the society. Thus the educational system not only held the gateway to the mainstream, but it also defined that mainstream to newcomers so that they could participate in it.

But the radical movements demanding that the gate be held open for all were at the same time demanding that definitions of success, basic values, and goals be reassessed. They defined the single view of the ladder as a denial of the basic rights of each group to have its own culture, its own definitions of success. In fact, many would claim that right for each individual rather than just for particular groups. Secure enough in their own family status, radical students wanted their education to enrich their personal lives rather than prepare them for places in a system they had come to distrust. They wanted that enrichment for others who had been held out of the mainstream but did not want them shaped to the values of the mainstream. Without realizing it, they universalized their own social and psychological needs, prescribing for others the goals and values they found important. But since their needs were primarily for freedom, they also demanded that the goals and values of each cultural and ethnic group be affirmed—at least as long as they were not those of the despised mainstream. While demanding that the rewards of the society be open to all, they were doing their best to define those rewards as worthless.

In their disaffection from the society, they wanted the schools to stress the mistakes and hypocrisies of the society rather than the myths that had defined it. Qualifying tests or other demonstrations of ability to fill jobs or enter classrooms were to be done away with since they were tools of discrimination. That they could also be rewards, signals of success to newcomers to the process, was a fact that escaped many of the cultural rebels. The ambivalence of the movement was that it sought to open doors to processes of advancement it hoped to destroy.

Underlying the ambivalence was the assumption that the schools should not be purveyors of a particular value system because that would inevitably favor the interest of one group over others. Neither should the economic system be the arbiter of social values. The government should protect the right of each group and individual to exercise its own life-style and to observe its own set of values, but it should never impose standards on people. Families were suspect sources of value since their traditional function had been to socialize their children to become accepting members of the "system."

Yet there seemed to be something missing, something related to the ability to express and celebrate the values of the movement. Historically, religion has provided that function. For many of these young people, the secularity of the educational system had left out any consideration of religion; so that alienation from it was not particularly deep-rooted. They had been too little involved in religion for alienation to have taken place in many of the young, except for a deep suspicion of the institutional church. Since religion is a common source of values, it is not difficult to see how many of the young radicals eventually turned to some form of it, though seldom to the churches that were part of the "system." But to understand the nature of the new religiosity, it is necessary that we trace some of the religious antecedents of the period.

Chapter 3

Religion for a Dislocated Generation

Some reference has been made to the place and the style of the churches in the post-World War II era. It is time now to take a second look, with a particular focus on their programs for children and youth during that period, as well as at other forms of religion that developed among the young people who were their natural clientele.

Postwar Religious Education

As members of the postwar baby boom crowded into classrooms in the schools, they also flocked to the Sunday schools, creating a demand for increased facilities that became part of the great expansion of the churches in the 1950s. In many areas churches moved faster than public boards of education to meet the needs for educational space. New church buildings with large education wings became a common sight in the suburbs.

Inside the classrooms, however, the adjustment was not always so swift, and an inevitable clash of teaching styles developed. On the one side stood traditional Sunday school teachers, accustomed to direct discussion of Bible stories and simple moral applications of biblical passages taught out of books or materials that required little methodological sophistication, planning, or preparation by teachers. Developed at a time when religious language and Bible reading at home complemented a consensual moral universe, this teaching style had served generations of church people and offered significant opportunities for participation in the education of the young by persons without formal teacher training.

On the other side of the argument could be found a growing cadre of specialists in religious education, trained in newer techniques of teaching and the psychological theory that underlay them. They were concerned that both the methods and the materials used in the church school be of equal or superior quality to those of the public schools. Materials they developed required trained teachers, and teacher training programs were developed through the denominations to prepare church volunteers to use them effectively. The new materials were, of course, considerably more expensive, a fact less threatening to thriving suburban churches than to many of the rural and inner-city congregations whose membership was diminished by the population shift. Again, the idea of professionalism in religious education was consistent with taken-for-granted expectations of specialization in the suburbs.

Yet in other ways the suburban style of life undercut the new forms of religious education. The sheer mobility of the suburban population made it difficult to train and keep an adequate volunteer teaching staff in the church schools or to count on student preparation for particular levels of learning in a cumulative curriculum. But even more of a problem as a religious style identified by Orr and Nichelson in *The Radical Suburb* was that of "expansive man." They compared the "expansive" style with two earlier ones. The first, the "savage," was based on fierce loyalty to the group, a stereotype of ethnic religion that emphasized maintaining boundaries around the religious fellowship. The second, the "conscientious," was grounded in a sense of moral obligation often identified with the Protestant Ethic.[1] In either of these styles the reliability of volunteer church workers could be assured. But the "expansive" style of the suburbs called for less serious loyalty, a willingness to experiment and move out into new areas, that tended to erode a specific commitment to programs and congregations. An expansive suburban population had outgrown the simplistic materials that required little training or regular preparation; yet their life-style demanded materials that could be used in that fashion. Furthermore, students in the classes, living expansively, tended not to be particularly regular in attendance or to appreciate having to do homework or serious study. Parents, more than ever living within the assumptions of a society of specialists, were not very supportive of programs that expected religious education to extend into the home, and the secularity of the culture precluded religious language as a common factor. As a result, in spite of dedicated efforts by many teachers and specialists, the quality of religious education in the churches tended not to be high. Many young people grew up not taking the churches very seriously, seeing them as ineffective organizations primarily concerned with suburban sociability and shallow conformity. Others who may have grown up in churches more oriented to the loyalistic or moralistic patterns frequently found themselves rebelling against religious strictures as they moved out into a society that no longer supported such styles.

The Secularization of Society

As neighborhoods became more heterogeneous, they lost the religious uniformity that had once underlain the views of the world expressed in the teaching of the neighborhood school. Family religious teaching could no longer be assumed to complement and be complemented by school activities such as Christmas pageants and Easter decorations. In the name of the separation of church and state many families protested such activities when they conflicted with their own religious practices. Some churches even took up the battle against religious expressions in public schools, fearing that the influence of an eclectic civil religion might dilute the more specific training they were trying to provide their young people. All these local influences complemented the influence of the secular humanism of the universities. In schools that we have seen tend to dominate the lives of young people, religion was not a factor to be considered. Many young people grew up assuming that the religious dimension was irrelevant in human life. What they did learn about religion in school tended to be negative. History taught them of the ways in which religion in the past had served as the motivation for particularly brutal warfare. Social studies taught how religion aided the poor to cope with an existence empty of other gratifications. The findings of social scientists who studied the relation of religious belonging to social class tended to support Marx's definition of religion as both an opiate of the masses and a tool of the powerful.

The experience of these young people with social institutions tended to support a negative assessment of religion. For many who had received religious training, it came to them as something imposed from the outside rather than in a way by which they could personally appropriate it. Those who grew up in ethnic enclaves or in the isolation of homogeneous communities often were initiated into what Orr and Nichelson called "savage" religion, a tight mold of loyalties and rigid roles that had to be transcended if they were to move out into the new world of the mid-twentieth century. Others, trained in the strict moralisms and obligations of the "conscientious" style, found such strictures offensive in their now-pluralistic environment, assuming that they were devised simply to keep adherents from challenging the status quo or upsetting the ordered lives of their elders. Those—perhaps the majority—whose experience of the church was in the "expansive" style often had the impression that religion was primarily a cynical and hypocritical form of social control. So much of the churchgoing in the suburbs was child-centered, and so many of them were enrolled in church school by parents who themselves did not attend, that students could easily come to believe that their religious education was one more plot by the adult world to fit them into a constricting social mold.

Often such definitions were encouraged by educators. For many academics, secular education had been the agent of liberation from savage or conscientious religious styles. The kinds of narrow contentiousness they remembered from their religious background represented the forces of ignorance and prejudice they hoped to overcome in their students, and this was reflected in their teachings, implicitly if not openly. Even religious teachers, in many cases, had come through similar battles in their personal histories and were concerned lest they lay similar strictures on the next generation in the name of a Christianity they now understood to be liberating. Often they did not have the words, the developed theologies, to teach their open view of the faith; so they said little, hoping to express in their style of working with the young the sense of Christianity's true essence, its message of love and liberation.

By the early 1960s theologians were attempting to deal with a religious faith in a secular age. They found in the Christian tradition ideological support for secularization. Harvey Cox, for example, in *The Secular City* traced three sources of secularization to early portions of the Old Testament. In the story of creation, he said, the world of nature was desacralized, treated as merely the handiwork of God rather than the sacred dwelling of the ancient gods of pantheism. The Exodus story, according to Cox, desacralized politics by showing divine support to a rebellion against a Pharaoh who claimed to rule as a god. Finally, in the giving of the Ten Commandments, Cox found the desacralization of religion itself, in that he interpreted the prohibition against worshiping anything of human creation to apply to creeds, priesthoods, and rituals, as well as idols of wood, stone, or metal.[2]

Cox's book was probably the most influential in the society because it was more popularly written than many others. However, secular theology became a popular force, and many people heard of, even if they did not understand, the theology of the "death of God." Christian theologians denied that Christianity was a religion in the ordinary sense but claimed instead that it was a way of living in the secular world. In general, theologians were wrestling with the question of Dietrich Bonhoeffer on how one speaks of God in a secular way.[3]

On the whole, however, these intellectual struggles in theological circles did not result in clear formulations that could be used effectively in the local church. Rather, particularly for young people during this period, the churches seemed merely to be supporting the impression that they had received in their secular studies—that religion had nothing to say to the lives of contemporary people.

The Visionary Quest

Few young people had learned about other definitions of the function of religion, about its place in helping to shape one's identity, about religious vision as a source of hope, a place from which to reconstruct human culture with the power of transcendent ideals. Few had read such social scientists as Max Weber, who showed the importance in human history of the visionary prophets, around whom social movements had coalesced to change both religious institutions and the societies around them. And yet, particularly for those most involved in the counterculture, this visionary social reconstruction was their need and their goal.

The vision quest had been a part of the turn to drugs. Their "mind-expanding" properties had allowed people to perceive new realities in their lives and surroundings, to understand experientially that the "social construction of reality"[4] is just that, that experience could be fitted into different patterns with different interpretations than those they had been taught. But the drug "trip" is essentially a private exercise, even when supported by group activities. To create a new culture, there had to be ways of communicating and sharing visions. Many drug culture communes broke up because there was no way of sharing in the practice of allowing each to do his or her own thing. At the same time, some drug-related experiences were akin to religious experience. They created a sense of awe in the presence of that which could not be explained but seemed to offer a new way of seeing the world that needed symbols or rituals to be communicated.

Eventually there developed among many young people in the counterculture a sort of formless religiosity. The old religious symbols were tainted with the general suspicion of institutions and with the secularity of many of their proponents. These young people were coming face to face with the sacred but without cultural tools to deal with it. The music began to reflect this. For example, singer Buffy Ste. Marie put to music lines of Leonard Cohen in a haunting song called "God Is Alive, Magic Is Afoot," with lines such as these:

God is alive. Magic is afoot. . . .
God is afoot. God never died.
God was ruler though his funeral lengthened.
Though his mourners thickened Magic never fled.
Though his shrouds were hoisted the naked God did live.
Though his words were twisted the naked Magic thrived.
Though his death was published round and round the world
The heart would not believe. . . .

Many strong men lied.
They came to God in secret and though they left him nourished
They would not tell who healed.
Though mountains danced before them they said that God was dead.
Though his shrouds were hoisted the naked God did live. . . .[5]

At the peak of their popularity the Beatles went to India in search of a guru, seeking in the East a religious sensibility they could not find in the West. While at one time one of their number had irreverently observed that they were more popular than Jesus Christ, they now wrote a new hit, "My Sweet Lord," dedicated not to Jesus but to the Lord Krishna. Perhaps one of the most explicit examples of the alienation from religion and yet the need for it could be found in some of the songs of the hard rock group, Jethro Tull. Their picture of the human condition in modern society may be seen in words from their "Slipstream":

Well the lush separation enfolds you—
and the products of wealth
push you along the bow wave
of their spiritless undying selves.
And you press on God's waiter your last dime—
as He hands you the bill,

and you spin in the slipstream
tideless—unreasoning—
paddle right out of the mess.

On institutional religion, Jethro Tull put forth this in the song "My God":

People—what have you done—
Locked Him in His golden cage.
Made Him bend to your religion—
Him resurrected from the grave. . . .

Or in "Hymn 43":

Oh Father high in heaven
smile down upon your son
who's busy with money games
his women and his gun.
And the unsung Western Hero
killed an Indian or three
and made his name in Hollywood
to set the white man free.
If Jesus saves—well
He'd better save Himself
from the gory glory seekers
who use His name in death.
I saw Him in the city
and on the mountains of the moon—
his cross was rather bloody
He could hardly roll His stone.[6]

© Copyright 1971, Chrysalis Music Ltd. Controlled in the U.S. and Canada by Rare Blue Music, Inc. Used by permission of the publisher. All Rights Reserved.

The "New Religions"

For many in the counterculture, the attempt to meet the religious needs that surfaced in alienation from institutional religion began with experimentation in various occult practices. Ancient methods of dealing with mystery were rediscovered. If Christianity was seen as the oppressor, then perhaps the ancient religions once conquered by that faith were the true way. In a time when life seemed unpredictable, the counterculture turned to tarot cards or the castings of the ancient Chinese I Ching for clues to the future. Having foregone most of the marks of social identification, they embraced astrology at least to the point of identifying one another according to zodiac signs and the character traits supposedly attached to them. Or they sought to recapture the conquered religions of Native Americans, seeing good rather than evil in treating nature as sacred in itself. Witchcraft was resurrected from secular histories that had defined it as hysteria or from religious equations of it with Satanism. In addition to being mysterious, it was found to contain surprisingly modern elements of concern for nature and equality of the sexes.

Some young people for whom these arcane pursuits seemed too far removed from modern life sought instead more contemporary religious expressions in non-Western cultures. The trip of the Beatles to India was part of a great migration of many young people to Eastern centers of religious teaching and practice. In return, a significant number of Eastern religions were brought to America, though usually not in pristine form. As Harvey Cox—still abreast of the latest religious sensibilities—wrote in his *Turning East,* the cultural prism through which these young Americans have viewed the Eastern religions has often distorted them beyond all recognition.[7] One common development has been the adaptation of some Eastern traditions to technological culture. For example, Transcendental Meditation was brought to this country by the Maharishi Mahesh Yogi, to whom followers gave traditional reverence as the guru of the movement. That, and the giving of a mantra as a focus of meditation, seemed to be the extent of traditionalism in TM, as it has been called. Scientific studies have been produced to show reduction in blood pressure and similar physiological benefits of meditative practices taught—for a fee—by TM trainers. Business corporations have been solicited (sometimes successfully) to enroll harassed executives in a TM course in order to increase their effectiveness in the organization. Many individuals similarly have undergone the training in a very secular search for techniques that could assist them in coping with a high-pressure society.

The more sophisticated and demanding disciplines of such traditions as Zen Buddhism have also often been corrupted, so that an attempt to lose the self becomes a way of finding oneself. Nichiren Shoshu Buddhism has sometimes been hawked on street corners as a way to get whatever you want merely by joining in the sacred chant of "Nam-myoho-renge-kyo." Yoga, rather than a total ascetic way of life, has become a series of exercises to be imitated when presented on TV or taught in school physical education classes. The secular touch of a technological society has tended to transmute any new religious quest into new and less "religious" forms with amazing speed, so that they become mere techniques for self-improvement.

It is hardly surprising, then, that many new forms of religion have become more strict, drawing boundaries around their adherents to protect them from secular influences. This more sectarian form of religion could be found in both Eastern and Western styles. The International Society of Krishna Consciousness, better known as the Hare Krishna people, offers perhaps the best example of Eastern sectarianism. While they have been quite open to visitors to their ashrams and festivals, the "bridge-burning" activities required of converts have set up barriers to their interaction with others as anything other than representatives of the group. The saffron robes and shaved heads of the men, long saris of the women, their practice of public solicitation of funds have all set them off from the rest of society with forms of "mental" and social isolation.[8] Their defenses against the influence of secular society have been at least as high as those raised in that society by their presumed deviant behavior.

Solicitation activities but not dress have set off from the rest of the society such other groups as the Unification Church of Sun Myung Moon (the "Moonies"). Their separateness has been marked by communal life-styles, and again the society has reinforced their isolation by defining Moon as a dangerous manipulator of his followers. The Moon organization has developed a complicated theology that combines Christian and Eastern elements, seeks to unify the perspectives of religion and science, and bases its hope on a new messiah, the Lord of the Second Advent. They have stopped just short of publicly proclaiming Moon to be that messiah, since it is believed that the Lord of the Second Advent will only be revealed as he effectively unifies the earthly life of the human race in its political, economic, and cultural expressions and transforms human families into perfect replicas of the divine dynamics of love.

Another form of religiosity more fully within the Christian framework has been the Jesus Movement in its various forms. This movement took up the countercultural criticism of modern culture, basing its critique on biblical ethics. Usually communal in life-style, Jesus Movement groups held to a literal reading of Scripture and an ascetic discipline while still maintaining such accoutrements of the counterculture as its style of dress and hair length as well as its musical styles. Some segments of the movement have spun off into highly authoritarian sects, hardly recognizable as related to their roots in evangelical Christianity. The Children of God, led by Moses Berg, have probably departed furthest from traditional Christian teaching, so much so that they have found it necessary to remove their central base of operations from America to Europe where dissenting religion is less expected to conform to social norms. Another authoritarian spin-off has established congregations scattered around the United States, first claiming to be a religious order under the name of the New Covenant Apostolic Order and more recently defining itself as a denomination, the Orthodox Evangelical Church. Leaders of this group, themselves dropouts from the conservative Campus Crusade for Christ who were looking for a continuation of involvement beyond the campus, have made extensive study of the ancient church fathers in order to try to reconstitute the ancient church as it was before the split between Rome and Constantinople. The authority and orthodoxy they have claimed are rigid enough to have already precipitated purges within the leadership over doctrinal matters.

But many of the Jesus Movement groups were less rigidly structured and were gradually absorbed into conservative congregations in areas where they could be found, often to become essentially the youth program of those churches. In fact, some students of the movement have defined its function for many members as that of providing an avenue of reentry into mainstream society from the counterculture.[9] Some of these former "Jesus freaks" now swell the ranks of the "young evangelicals," who combine conservative theology with cogent cultural criticism, seeking to reform the society in the name of Christ.[10]

The new religions, like most social movements, have spawned countermovements as well, particularly in this case a broadly based and widespread "anticult" movement. The first highly publicized group was composed of parents of recruits to the Children of God, who formed FREECOG, an acronym for "Free Our Children from the Children of God." Since that time parents' oranizations have taken up the fight against Jesus Movement groups, Moon's Unification Church, Hare Krishna, and a host of others, including occasionally any slippage from the family's traditional religion. The movement has developed a leadership of professional "deprogrammers" who have been accused of manipulative practices akin to those with which some "cult" leaders have been charged. Indeed, their ideology assumes that members of the new movements have been "brainwashed"; so that the only way to get them out is to reverse the process by "deprogramming," sometimes with the use of force. Indeed, some members of this movement, both distraught parents and deprogrammed youth, give the appearance of fanaticism that seems itself religious, leading some observers to classify the anticult movement with the new religions.

Sources of the Movement Toward "New Religions"

Many more groups could be mentioned here, both those explicitly religious and those more in line with the transpersonal psychologies mentioned as part of the campus scene. But what is more important than describing the characteristics of specific groups is to notice the variety of them and the fact that new ones have kept springing up. This gives evidence of the fact that the primary causes of the new religions are not just their recruitment methods, their leaders, or their ideolo-

Religion for a Dislocated Generation 77

gies, but rather factors within the society itself. Their existence raises some salient questions: Why this surge of religiosity; why the need to be religious outside the forms of religion already provided by the society? At a time when everyone, even the churches, seemed to accept the direction of human history to be toward secularization, how can such an outburst of religion be understood? What have all these new forms of religiosity to do with traditional American religion as we have known it? Do they point toward fundamental changes in the churches, or do they constitute a passing phase, to be ignored until it goes away? Certainly many young people have become involved in these groups and then moved out into an ordinary secular life. Are these groups then ephemeral?

This is certainly not the first time in American history when there has been a lush outcropping of popular religiosity. Embedded in the very foundation of the nation are the effects of the "Great Awakening." Perhaps one of the most important contributions made by that movement was a sense of independence from European religious roots that helped lay foundations for the thinking of political independence. Later "awakenings" and the spate of religious movements arising out of such areas as the "burnt-over district" of the eastern Great Lakes region have contributed new religious movements to the culture, many of which have resulted in denominations or groups still part of modern American society. Even the current interest in Eastern religions has been predated by some movements earlier in this century. A high percentage of the membership of past movements has come from economically or culturally marginal people—the poor, the disenfranchised, or those whose affluence has lifted them out of the bustling mainstream of American life without firmly placing them in some valued social role.

In the modern scene we may again trace the source of new religions to cultural marginality, this time focused on a particular age group that was in a position to see itself cut off from full participation in American institutional life. Most movements of the past also have had in their numbers a disproportionate percentage of the young; they are the ones with fewer direct and demanding ties to structures of family, economy, or other institutions. Seldom, however, have such movements been so identified with just that one age group. Whether or not the reputation is accurate, it is based on one factor that is significant—the size of the age cohort that fit the category of "youth" during the later 1960s and early 1970s. As we shall see later, this fact points to a future that may continue to be dominated by that particular age cohort through the next several decades. Another unique characteristic of the present movement is its location primarily among the young of the more privileged sectors of the society. It seems to have been those from families most affected by a rapid rise in social class and life-style who have been most prone to the new religiosity. These young people, for the most part, have not sought religion as a compensation for economic lack or low status. Those suffering such social disabilities have been far more susceptible to political movements, far less critical of traditional avenues to social mobility such as access to educational programs. Adherents to the new religions have tended to come from segments of the society for whom traditional avenues of success have worked but seem not to have provided a satisfactory life.

One way of understanding this has been through the insights of developmental psychology. In recent years considerable attention has been given the work of such psychologists as Erik Erikson, Abraham Maslow, Jean Piaget, Lawrence Kohlberg, and James Fowler that takes seriously the place of moral and religious development in the growth of the human personality. Several elements of these developmental patterns seem particularly relevant here. First is the basic assumption that, while certain stages of psychological or moral development are commonly linked to particular age levels in recognition of the importance of elements of physical and social maturation, these stages are also understood to be sequential. That is, no matter what a person's age, he or she cannot truly reach a later state of psychological, moral, or religious development without first successfully passing through earlier stages.

Thus, a beginning point of the developmental journey is a sense of basic trust, a perception of the world as relatively predictable and benevolent, ideally attained during infancy. However, for many children disruptions in the family and the community have made such a perception of the world problematic. An example is the response of a teenager to a questionnaire item on important incidents in his life:

My father and mother getting divorced.
My father marrying my stepmother.
My father divorcing my stepmother.
When my father married my second stepmother,
I felt nothing.
When my brother left home, I felt angry.
When I found Jesus, I felt relief.

It seems clear in this case that only in the conservative Christian group in which he was now a member had he begun to feel that sense of trust basic to further development. Given the kinds of massive dislocation suffered by families and individuals in the past decades, it may be assumed that this young man's experience was not highly unusual. Here the religious group can serve as a surrogate family, providing the basis for further growth. Not only is this a factor in the age group under consideration here, but it seems also to be an important factor among the next younger age cohort, perhaps even with greater intensity.

For those who were part of the postwar baby boom, two other segments of developmental theory also seem particularly relevant. In Erikson's work, for example, a stage usually associated with adolescence is one which allows the young to move their identities beyond the narrow circle of family and neighborhood by offering them a coherent, if simplified, view of the meaning of life and their place in it—an ideology.[11] Religious institutions have long given recognition to this stage through initiation rites and puberty rituals that celebrate the ideology of the group and provide occasions for public demonstration of a young person's commitment to it. In the churches this has been found in confirmation services or in conversion and baptism services in those traditions that accept only adult commitment to the faith. In either case, what is offered is some presentation of the major outlines of the faith, along with a ritual means of declaring one's allegiance to it in a public act. Such a ritual not only provides the ideological component for the emerging adult commitment of the young person, but also reenacts the commitment of older members of the group, pulling them and the initiate into a sense of community around shared values that are an important basis for social identity and participation.

In recent decades, particularly in churches with a relatively liberal theology, there has been considerable pulling back from such rituals of commitment. In their desire to make sure that religious belonging is truly voluntary rather than a response to social pressure, church leaders have downplayed the experiential and ritualistic aspects of the faith, emphasizing instead rational approaches that should support an informed commitment to the faith. Cautious of oversimplifying Christianity in ways that would not be true to its full reality, they have presented it cautiously, in a style far less gripping than many incidental aspects of the lives of the young, such as sports or rock music, for example. Young people who learn the faith in that way are often simply bored by it rather than inspired to commitment. Thus their turn to other religions or to more conservative Christian groups may be seen as a search for ideology necessary to their stage of social and moral development.

The second aspect of the stage theory of moral development that is particularly applicable to this situation has to do with the expectation that a person, after developing a sense of loyalty to and identity in some social group, will need to move beyond unreasoning commitment to its ideology to some questioning of its meaning to that person's life, out of personal experience and reflection. In most liberal churches it has been taken for granted that by mid- or late adolescence young people are ready for this kind of activity, and youth groups and campus ministries have been developed which allow young people to draw back somewhat from active participation in the community of faith into a position where they can look critically at current practices. Under the right circumstances, this has encouraged reform in the churches, enlisting young idealists in processes that both improve the witness of organized religion and weld young people into the community of believers as leaders committed to the faith. For example, anyone who knows of the peak period of the Student Christian Movement and the church leaders it has produced must be impressed with the value of that movement to organized religion.

But for the age cohort that reached high school and college in the late 1960s and early 1970s, it seems evident that all too often the critical questioning was encouraged before the basic commitments had been formed. Rather than a source of meaning and identity, the church became for many of these young people simply one more oppressive social institution, demanding loyalty and obedience for reasons of institutional survival rather than as part of one's personal life-style. Thus meaning and identity must be sought by this age cohort, if at all, in groups not part of the religious "establishment."

Church Involvement in the Youth Culture

Many of the youth and campus ministries of the churches sought to approach young people on their own "turf" during the period of their most agonized separation from the rest of the society. In doing so, they often increased their own separation from the ongoing life of the remainder of the church.

A telling example of this could be seen in the action of many campus ministers in particular, during the activist years of the sixties and seventies. Campus ministry by that time had developed something of a life of its own. In order to give college students the freedom to question, that they were understood to need, and yet to leave local congregations free enough of the questioners so that they could continue to teach and nourish other age groups, churches provided special clergy on campuses. These were usually responsible to wider segments of the church than local congregations, just as students came from wider areas than a single parish. By the late

1960s, most campus ministries of main-line denominations were administered through United Ministries in Higher Education (UMHE), an ecumenical organization sponsored by such national denominations as the American Baptists, United Church of Christ, United Presbyterian, Southern Presbyterian, Episcopal, Disciples of Christ, the United Methodist, and the Reformed Church in America. Lutheran campus ministries, administered by a board uniting the work of major Lutheran bodies, generally cooperated with those in UMHE, and on most campuses many projects were run cooperatively by Protestant, Catholic, and Jewish campus ministers. In the stronghold of secular humanism that most universities had become, traditional divisions between religious groups were too expensive and embarrassing to be honored. Denominational labels were generally treated as symbols of a narrowness to be overcome by education.

The type of person most suited to campus ministry was one whose commitment to a particular congregation or denomination had been transcended in a realization of more universal values shared by many traditions. Given this background, they tended to be more comfortable working alone, in their own style, rather than in close harmony with some ecclesiastical organization. Campus ministers also needed to possess a high level of intellectual skill as apologists for the faith in an intellectual community. In fact, in a study done by Phillip Hammond in the 1960s, many campus ministers were found to aspire to faculty status, saying they would be at least as happy as professors as they were as ministers.[12] In both their institutional placement and their personal values, campus ministers tended to have loyalties divided between church and college, and so did many of the church members on campus whom they served. Often, indeed, some campus ministers expressed greater identity with persons in their programs who were not active church members than with those actively loyal to their own denomination.

During the earlier 1960s, when the primary form of religious social activism was found in the civil rights struggle, campus ministers and denominational staff persons were highly overrepresented in freedom rides and demonstrations. But at that time there was widespread agreement among church leaders that racial justice was a proper concern of Christian ethics. Later in the decade, when campus concerns appeared more closely allied to political left wing movements and couched in Marxist rhetoric, more effort was needed to relate the causes to traditional Christian concerns. This was probably particularly true because of the isolated position in the society of the campuses and their young residents. But at that time many campus ministers became so caught up in the movements on campus that they no longer took the time to translate their rhetoric into traditional Christian themes. The definition of older people as the enemy became a barrier between the campus ministries and church congregations and denominations.

A pair of examples from the West Coast may serve to show how this process occurred. In Berkeley, as the counterculture grew and the town became a magnet for disaffected young people, it became evident that many of these migrants needed shelter. The University of California campus was a target of their attraction, at least partly because campuses were expected to be sanctuaries from a hostile society. One of the services offered students there by UMHE had been a communal living center known as the Briar Patch. In the division of labor among campus ministers, this program was the responsibility of the Methodist minister, though it occupied Presbyterian property. Students there, in true communal style, had governed themselves, and they now agreed to admit some of the rootless young people seeking shelter. As more and more came, democratic decision making was strained by their lack of responsibility to the community. Eventually the place became noted as one of the primary drug markets in Berkeley, a disorderly house full of careless young people and dogs, a public nuisance. The Presbyterian owners of the facility eventually closed the Briar Patch to any and all residents. It did not help in the process that the responsible person there was a minister of another denomination, less known to Presbyterian officials, with little or no fund of goodwill within the denomination on which to draw.

Across the Bay, at San Francisco State, a bitter strike of students and teachers against an administration willing to call in police to break up meetings found an off-campus base in Ecumenical House, a center of UMHE, Lutheran, and Jewish campus ministries and also at the Catholic Newman Center there. When university officials asked the churches to close down the centers, church officials did support their campus ministers. However, local church people tended to take sides against the strikers and to question the campus ministers' support of the movement. Later, some of the ministers reported that they were not sure that they had not been used by movements that shared little of their value base. Yet even at that later time, one faculty member at San Francisco State defined the centers as "islands of humanity, of love and concern, in a sea of impersonality and regimentation." Again, one may see the gap in perception between campus and the churches that seemed to result in the abrogation of mutual responsibility between campus ministries and those who sponsored them.

In many areas by the 1970s many of the campus ministers found themselves essentially bereft of clientele. Churches which had supported them through UMHE and had allowed that organization to serve as a buffer between them and some of the uncomfortable issues campus ministers were likely to raise now found it easy to withdraw support from ministries they had never directly claimed. Campus radicals used their facilities and their good name, then moved on in their own direction, without ever sharing important goals with the ministries. A new generation of students, less alienated from religious institutions, had not heard of campus ministries through their congregations and sought out local congregations for any religious involvment they chose to have during their college years. At best, they tended to view campus ministries as agencies of a failed revolution in which they had no part.

Thus at a time when young people were seeking commitments within a framework of experience and value traditionally defined as religious but were also in rebellion against institutional religion, the primary agencies that churches had developed to turn that rebellion to commitment were not in a position to speak forcefully for the churches. They had lost contact with the institution and with the rebelling young.

Commitment, Community, and the Churches

It is not appropriate to ask campus ministries to bear all the blame for their failure. The basis upon which they were shaped assumed a process of Christian formation in local congregations that would provide committed Christian young people ready now to question how well the churches were living up to their own values. In reality, however, we have seen that many local churches allowed the kind of critical stance espoused in secular education to dominate their teaching of the young; so that commitment tended always to be conditional. For some young people, perhaps the most idealistic, this was interpreted as a lack of power and relevance in Christianity. To those young people, the assurance evidenced by conservative Christians or new messiahs or the novelty of non-Western religions was particularly attractive.

One of the primary attractions of many new religious movements was the sense of community developed within them, usually experienced as a socially isolated community of the young. Main-line religion had done little to counteract the prevailing social mood of the time that defined young people as a group set apart from the rest of the society, often in opposition to other age groups. Given assumptions of the developmental stage of youth that underlay most youth and campus ministries, little effort was put forth to make the young a dynamic part of the ongoing life of local congregations. In fact, most of them had experienced a separation from congregational life from their earliest years. Religious educators, concerned that the young learn their faith in a manner consistent with their developing intellects, had dismantled many of the communal aspects of church schools. For example, old-fashioned "opening exercises" that brought together young and old for prayer, songs, and such acts of recognition as special birthday offerings were decried as oversimplified for older members, meaningless to the younger. Instead, each age group was encouraged to use the entire time available for activities appropriate to their level of understanding, already too short to provide the kind of instruction really needed. Such changes were quite appropriate to theories of learning but tended to ignore other, less cognitive aspects of religious ritual. Children growing up in such church schools, brought into the full congregational community only for formal worship (if that), had no experience of personal participation in an intergenerational community of shared values. When they began to perceive the need for community, it could hardly be expected that they would look beyond the bounds of their own age group. Consequently, they were attracted to religious organizations predominantly, if not exclusively, composed of the young.

In that practice young people were merely reflecting trends common in the society at large, including its churches. As settlement patterns became more urban but also more broadly spaced within sprawling metropolitan areas, it became easier for persons to see and know only people of similar background, living in houses of comparable size and price, near schools, churches, and shopping centers that served their particular life-style. Transportation to the workplace from these relatively isolated living areas was most commonly obtained by way of private automobiles hurrying along expressways not calculated to offer genuine glimpses of housing and life-styles of other groups. Thus metropolitan living, instead of encouraging a kind of cosmopolitan acceptance of a variety of cultural styles, tended to replace the ethnic exclusiveness of earlier "urban villagers" with an equally exclusive view of the world based more on social class. Churches may have tried to teach a more universal faith, but in their congregational life they most often simply reinforced the uniformity of life-style in their neighborhood, to the exclusion of other ways of living. The counterculture was a rebellion against that uniformity, but it often developed its own patterns of conformity, becoming one more isolated segment of a society growing less pluralistic in the true sense and more fragmented. Each of the new religions tended to become the expression of an isolated group of the young related only in the eyes of those outside the youth culture who tended to lump them all together as deviant and dangerous.

It must be remembered that the primary foci of meaning and value for most of the young of this period, in spite of the traditionally religious function they served, were secular. Those most oriented toward public values tended to be caught up with religious fervor in the political movements of the time. As immersed in Marxist rhetoric as their fundamentalist cohorts were in Scripture, they devoted themselves to the salvation of society through revolution. Again, like many religious groups, they often defined themselves as the only bearers of social salvation, an elite held apart from the uncommitted masses. Other young people, intent on the search for the self, utilized the methods of humanistic psychology to enhance their aims. For many, this resulted in a kind of individualism that admitted no loyalty or responsibility to larger social groups. Both these styles were encouraged in some ways within the church at large and perhaps particularly in youth and campus ministries. Again, the specialization of those ministries worked against grounding either social activism or the search for the self in the community or the tradition of local Christian organizations.

The turn to religion by the young was in large part a search for grounded identity, community, and purpose in a society that had largely denied them the customary routes to such goals. They may have perceived a conspiracy as the cause of that denial, but it seems evident that it occurred primarily as a result of a combination of circumstances impossible to blame on any one source. They lived at a particular point in history where a confluence of events had served to make their experience uniquely problematic.

Chapter 4

A Unique Cohort?

For the person who tries to make sense out of social changes, one of the most important questions to ask of the information we have been considering has to do with the permanence of these trends. Is it likely that the experience of the particular age group under consideration will be repeated by the next age group or even intensified? Or is this a unique situation, unlikely to be repeated? What does this story of today's young adults tell us about the future?

Two truisms must be acknowledged at the beginning: There is nothing particularly unique about a younger generation being in conflict with their elders. And not all members of this age group were caught up in the events and attitudes we have dealt with here. Rather, the question is whether either the experiences or the numbers were significant enough to have a lasting impact on the society.

One other thing is evident: The revolution of the counterculture did not have the direct effect on the society that was predicted by its early proponents. The "greening of

America" cannot be said to have been accomplished; the land is still significantly and increasingly covered with concrete, and along with that symbolic sight we can find many other evidences of the failure of the counterculture to bring an immediate transformation to the society. Radical political movements are far less evident as we move into the eighties, though their aims seem not to have been accomplished. Centers of hippie culture, harbingers of the cultural revolution in the late 1960s, now have either reverted to their original populations or have retained leftover members of the "love generation" carrying on a life-style more like that of the traditional skid row than the joyous celebrations of their heyday. The larger society has absorbed most of the generation that so protested against it. Has this generation made a difference? Will it?

Defining a Generation

To understand the dynamics of what has happened, it may be necessary to explore in some depth some of the ideas of social theorists, particularly those of Karl Mannheim, who has done some interesting work on "the problem of generations."[1] He begins with the notion that while younger and older generations are contemporaries, exposed to some of the same historical occurrences, they experience them differently because they come at different points in the development of their life perspectives. After all, we do not just accumulate experiences in a heap; rather, they come to us sequentially. Early experiences go together to make up what we will ever after take to be the natural order of things. Things that happen later will, then, always be seen from the perspective of the earlier definitions, either confirming or negating our sense of natural order. Thus, the common location of people of the same age on this ladder of development of social awareness will incline generational groups toward similar definitions of any occurrence. For the young an occurrence may be taken as evidence of the very nature of reality, while for those who are older it may seem to be a temporary aberration or an expected movement along an already perceived path.

Yet no particular age group is uniform in the way its members experience an event. It also depends on their social location. By the time one has reached adolescence, a good deal of information has been learned, largely through parents and teachers or other older representatives of the society. What they teach varies according to the social location of the family and other groups that do the teaching. But each subgroup, each "generation unit," will have been equipped with a perceptual filter based on the traditions and experiences of people in their particular social location, whether that be defined as social class, ethnic group, place of residence, or some other factor. They will also be positioned in the society so that any contemporary event may affect them differently from people in another position, even if they are of the same age. Yet the perceptual filters they will have been given will never quite fit their own experience. In fact, one of the constant causes of tension between generations comes from adult teaching that, in order to provide appropriate socialization, deals with things as they *ought* to be rather than things as they *are*. Those who teach such ideals are easy targets, then, for accusations of hypocrisy from young people whose experience begins to refute the ideal picture that has been presented. However, says Mannheim, in times of rapid change there is a difference greater than this, one where there is a radical disjunction between the experiences of the generations.[2]

In any society at any one time, there are groups whose ideas reflect quite different options in the way they look at the world. The reaction to events may take a progressive, liberal cast where improvement, "progress," and change tend to be synonymous. American history has provided considerable grounding for this kind of response, with its emphasis on the future as the location of the ideal society people were trying to carve out of the wilderness. Yet there have always been people, too, who take what Mannheim has called a more "romantical" view, where change is treated as a threat; these persons spark movements to deny or reverse the trend. The social location of some people tends to fix them in the direction of one or the other of these responses, though there are always individuals who are in rebellion against the attitude most common in their particular social location. But the largest group that is inherently free to choose one option or the other, says Mannheim, is that of the intellectuals, the idea people who may be the very ones whose ability with words communicates the ideology of a group or a movement to the rest of the society.[3] The particular approach that at any time attracts the most of these idea people may come to seem the *Zeitgeist*—the spirit of the age. People whose vision is different may feel that they are somehow out of line with their age or with their peers.

Within any generation, then, its "spirit" may be seen not as the attitude of all its members but the dominant one, the one accepted and promoted by the media of the time, which sweeps other members of the age group along. Some members of the generation may protest, but their understanding of life and of themselves is colored by the popular definition of what their generation is, does, and believes. Thus, while at no time was there a statistical majority of youth in the late sixties and early seventies actively and significantly involved in the counterculture, it became the hallmark of their generation. Insofar as this is true, the actual percentage of people involved becomes immaterial. The events that produced political and cultural rebellion were the events of their time; and though they experienced them differently, they were common to all, occurring during their formative years. Whether they evaluated the popular response of their generation positively or negatively, it became the common definition of their identity to which they were bound to react.

Some people have said that the counterculture was merely a "media event." There is some truth to that, particularly in some of its more extreme aspects. However, one needs also to explore the ways in which the rebellions of the time attracted media attention and, more particularly, the blessing of much of the intellectual community. One may say that the counterculture became important only because of the heavy investment of Americans in television sets, for there was much of "show biz" in the style and tactics of both the political and the cultural rebellions of the time. But it would be a mistake to treat it at that shallow a level. There was some attractiveness about the movements that caught the imagination of more people than those actively involved, something that media exposure exploited but did not create.

There is, for example, considerable evidence that the disjuncture between the generations was unusually great at that time. For example, statistical evidence of that kind of break has been given by Robert Wuthnow in a study of the "religious consciousness" of residents of the San Francisco Bay area. On measures of religious belief and practice, he found a trend by age that clearly reversed between people of the age of thirty-five and older and those younger than thirty-five in 1973.[4] The relevance of this is startling when one computes that people thirty-five and older were born before World War II. Even if their fathers went to war and later attended college to participate in the "great migration," they would have done so only after having already made those commitments to the social order that are represented by marriage and having and supporting children. The social and geographic migration of these families would have been on the base of an already established social identity rather than the more fluid social position and personal identity already described as characteristic of younger families. People who were thirty-five or older in 1973 were, then, part of a generation whose family life may have reflected much more the experience of the Great Depression, with its emphasis on primary needs rather than on attitudes or perspectives of a postwar affluence. They also would have completed college before the movements of the 1960s began to set youth apart in the extreme way that they did. When the counterculture slogan of "Don't trust anyone over thirty!" was coined, these people were on the over-thirty side of that division, clearly identified with the oppressive world of the "establishment," even if they were only a few years older than the radicals.

Mannheim, in his discussion of generations as social phenomena rather than just biological turnover, stated that the period between generations depended upon events that might raise certain units of a generation to become symbols of a particular *Zeitgeist*. It took enough change to demand a new view of life before this could happen, he said. At the same time, some age groups can experience so much change that they never really develop an *entelechy*—an "expression of unity of inner aim—its inborn way of experiencing life and the world." Says Mannheim, "These generations, frustrated in their production of an entelechy, tend to attach themselves, where possible, to an earlier generation which may have achieved a satisfactory form, or to a younger generation which is capable of evolving a newer form."[5]

Is it not possible to see in the events of the 1950s and 1960s this process within the older generation, those who reached adulthood during or immediately after World War II? Dislocated in their own lives to the point that they may indeed have failed to produce any sense of unity of aim or way of experiencing life, but firm in their belief in progress, may not this age group have attached themselves to the younger generation, hopeful of their capacity for cultural reconstruction? Margaret Mead has already been quoted in this regard, but she was only one of the many intellectuals who looked to the young to lead the way into a future made incomprehensible to older members of the society. Such popular writers as Marshall McLuhan expounded theories about the different way of viewing life that was coming about in a generation formed by television rather than print. McLuhan predicted the loss of a straight-line view of history among those whose learning came exploding at them out of the TV set rather than in the sequential letters and lines of books,[6] and indeed the counterculture (and most "straight" students of the time as well) evidenced a marked avoidance of historical perspectives. Marcuse's critique of the "one-dimensional man"[7] of modern society was taken up in many ways by the young of the period, who sought an end to the "single vision and Newton's sleep" of modern science.[8] Even such adult "squares" as Baptist minister Jess Moody were intrigued by the changes brought about in the multiplication of stimuli in the modern world:

When my father was eighteen, he was hit by an average of 800-1200 sensate impressions per day. A sensate impression is any impression made upon the senses. . . .

This is why the statement "When I was your age . . ." is dead. *There has never been a time when I was exactly the same age as my son!*

I was a 2200-3000 sensate impression eighteen-year-old and my son is a 16,000-22,000 sensate impression eighteen-year-old! I have never been and can never be a 16,000-22,000 sensate impression teenager. This is the reason my son finds it difficult to relate to my thought processes, to my life view.[9]

Much of the ideology swirling around the counterculture was apocalyptic. Jesus Movement groups were explicit in their statements that the end of the world was approaching, that Judgment Day was near. The Children of God paraded in sackcloth and ashes at sporting events, demanding that people repent before it was too late. Political protesters took for granted that we were on the verge of (1) being wiped out by all the people of the world whom we had subjected to colonial exploitation and oppression, (2) so defiling the earth with waste and overpopulation that there would soon be less than one square yard of standing room for each person on a totally garbage-covered planet, (3) blowing the whole thing to smithereens with an H-bomb or sentencing it to slow death through atomic radiation, or all of the above. Economic and social theorists discussed our arrival at a "postmodern" stage, where assumptions about the value of increased production would be challenged and a whole new way of evaluating human life would be required. More optimistic members of the counterculture consulted occult calendars and declared the dawning of the Age of Aquarius—an age of love, joy, and fellowship. What was common, what seemed indeed to be the *Zeitgeist*, was a conviction that we were at the end of an era, that if there was to be any future, it would have to be in the hands of those who were not locked into the old ways. And that conviction was found not only among the young but also among their mentors. Whether they wanted it or not, these youth were being handed the responsibility for the salvation of the world. There was a definition of the situation that demanded of their age group an *entelechy* for the entire age, that made them the people of a *generation* in the social-historical sense.

A Fatal Separation

However, there was an important link missing in the process by which these responsibilities were laid on the young. They may indeed have become convinced that they were harbingers of a new age. But the ways in which they were led to such a conviction were the paths of alienation and rebellion, experiences that taught them to define themselves in opposition to the rest of the society. There was little in their understanding of their place in the society to cause them voluntarily to pick up the burdens of the entire nation. If they sought enlightenment, it was for themselves. If they tried to build alternate communities, they were communities of the young, not intergenerational ones. They may have widely used a rhetoric of worldwide love and brotherhoood, but in practice it was a community of a single-age cohort that they considered capable of such high ideals.

Some of that lack of connectedness between themselves and the larger public could be traced to elements in the culture that have been endemic in American society, including its religious ethic. Max Weber, in his seminal work on the Protestant Reformation as well as his observations of Protestant sects in America, characterized the nature of both Protestantism as a whole and American religion in particular as that of "innerworldly asceticism." That is, he found the greatest emphasis to be on control of self and the environment for purposes of glorifying God through action in the world. The idea of personal asceticism for future benefit was seen by Weber as basic to the capitalistic economy, a religious motivation for people to save and invest rather than using their funds for immediate improvement in their style of life.[10] Nations whose ethic did not have this base found an alternative in state socialism, which in essence forced the kind of saving (through taxation) that could allow industrial development by the state rather than by the individual. One of the side effects of Protestant economic asceticism, in contrast to the socialist form, came from its equating of individual economic activity with religious merit. The public good was seen as an outgrowth of the individual pursuit of personal advancement defined as a righteous style of life rather than requiring collective decisions and plans.

While the utility of such an ethic has shrunk with the modernization of the economy, it still tends to underlie our sense of participation in the public realm. Ideals of democracy have made it inappropriate to teach public responsibility as behavior appropriate to one's "station." Yet notions of individual mobility as publicly valuable seem to have been most useful in societies engaged in economic development as we have known it. Once the basic tasks of development are taken care of, the pursuit of individual advancement is likely to become competitive for shares of a limited supply of goods and services or to require a constant manufacturing of new needs for the economy to supply that it may continue to operate at full capacity.

This generation was caught between an ethic of asceticism and the demand for consumption in order to keep the system working. They rebelled against a system that sought to enforce ascetic hard work in order to meet "need" created through advertising. In an affluent society they no longer felt the goad of poverty pushing them to work—particularly the middle-to-upper class youth who were in the forefront of the cultural rebellion. They felt entitled to a decent life-style, oppressed by those who demanded of them sacrifices to gain what was already available. Traditional values in the society tended to define public responsibility in terms of work and sacrifice. This generation, rejecting the forms of work they had perceived to be alienating as well as sacrifice that was defined as unnecessary, was in many ways rejecting the only paths to public responsibility provided them. Notions that they should provide new visions for the entire society, and should make sacrifices to communicate them, did not set well under the circumstances. Instead, they acted out their sense of entitlement, taking the actions and goods that they needed for their own life-style and letting it go at that.

Attempting to escape from the imprisoning walls of institutions that they felt were trying to turn them into what they were not, they took as their primary goal the discovery, development, and expression of the self innate in each person. They felt that group loyalties should hold only so long as they enhanced self-development. Marital commitments were to be avoided because of their potential power to inhibit the growth and expression of each partner's individuality. In speech, dress, actions, and friendships, individuality was to be prized.

They recognized the need for social reform but had little knowledge of or experience in the channels by which people have been able to make social changes. Their social studies in high school and college, rather than initiating them into the processes of public participation, had tended instead to emphasize a view of social determinism that only added to their sense of frustration. Their response, then, was either to pull away into their own private worlds or to express their frustrations in mass action intended to destroy the "system," with no plans to replace it with a better one.

The Rise of Religious Populism

Now the days of open rebellion are past, and some of the withdrawal has also dissolved. The age cohort has reentered the mainstream of the society, for the most part. There, however, the perceptions and experiences of their formative years must necessarily have an effect on the way in which they participate in the social order and so on the society itself. It becomes necessary, then, to look at current social trends with an eye to their possible relation to the earlier experiences of today's young adults, who make up such a large portion of the society because of the population bulge that they represent.

One such trend has been noted by Wuthnow, who also ties it to religious styles. That is a trend toward populism, which he defines thus:

> The distinguishing features of populism include: (1) a primary belief in the "intrinsic and immediate validity of the popular will," (2) fluid standards subject to fads and crazes, (3) diversity in ideas and organization . . . , (4) resentment of elites and elite intellec-

tuals, and (5) organizations that treat people as members of a mass audience or market.[11]

It is not hard to distinguish the shape of populism, thus defined, in many elements of current society. The contrast of the "popular will" with the "will" of big government, big education, big business, and the like, is a common theme, and rebellions within the ranks of most social institutions in the name of the people are common. Union locals rebel against the national organization. Voters petition to have put on the ballot laws that will limit the power and scope of government. The big corporation has become the whipping boy of consumers, workers, and regulators. People have become suspicious of national media, seeking out local systems of information or, more often, special networks of interest groups with which they identify.

It may be instructive to apply to religious behavior some of the features of populism mentioned by Wuthnow. Certainly in the many religious movements of our day we can find fads and crazes, with some people drifting quickly from one to another, as populism enters the public consciousness. There is little doubt of the diversity available in both ideas and organizations, and, of course, the accompanying rhetoric has been heavy with antiestablishment and anti-intellectual themes. It seems of particular interest that in the waning years of the decade of the 1970s the religious scene in general, not just among the young, has featured many elements of the other two factors, the mass marketing of religion and the assertion of the primacy of the popular will.

Perhaps the most obvious example of religion as a marketing phenomenon is found in the so-called electronic church. In recent years there has been phenomenal growth in religious programming on radio and television, with the development of a national religious broadcasting network as well as widespread distribution of religious messages by cassette tape. Talk shows, such as the "PTL Club" or the "700 Club," join worship services from the glass cathedral of Robert Schuller and the frequently broadcast evangelistic crusades of Billy Graham and Oral Roberts to reach a wide and varied audience of people who may or may not be regularly involved in local church congregatons. Local religious organizations are making use of the channels of cable TV to air their evangelistic messages, competing with some of the more established churches that have been broadcasting local services for years. A wide variety of churches offer "dial-a-prayer" or similar ministries by telephone.

The one thing in common to all these and a host of other electronic ministries is the acceptance of the style and basic assumptions of marketing theory in the public presentation of religion. This is nothing new in American religion, but it has never been so extensive, so pressing upon main-line Christianity to respond in kind rather than to write off such use of public media as the activity of fringe groups. It is probably no coincidence that this is occurring at a time when the generation labeled by Wuthnow as religious populists have become part of adult society.

There also appears to be some connection between the reabsorption of that generation into the society's mainstream and the resurgence of that segment of American Christianity which rebels against organized religion in the name of more localized forms. Much of this is interpreted as an increased interest in evangelical Christianity. Kelley finds the genius for the growth of conservative churches in their clear sense of religious identity, their discipline and commitment.[12] Others look at the kinds of market mentality mentioned above. The interest does not seem limited to disciplined groups of those specifically concerned with making converts. Much more common among growing churches is a strong local identification, a tendency to revolt against church bureaucrats in the same way that popular movements are condemning big government in Washington and the powerful organizations of multinational corporations. Denominations are having increasing problems with recalcitrant congregations that insist on supporting their own missionaries and worthy causes rather than those designated by the denomination. Many refuse to use educational materials supplied by the denomination or to provide support for regional or national staffs. While national efforts at ecumenical cooperation have stalled for lack of support, people have happily come together across denominational lines in local charismatic prayer groups. Sectarian groups once associated almost entirely with lower socioeconomic classes are common among more affluent groups, often composed mostly of young adults. Denominational campus ministries languish, while evangelical groups that make the local campus their focus seem to flourish.

All these trends seem to fit well into a definition of religious populism, which, as Wuthnow sees it, differs from pluralism in that it is not composed of clearly defined groups, each relatively separate, each treated as legitimate as a focus for loyalty and commitment. In religious populism, the boundaries are much less distinct than in pluralism, the traditions blurred, their authority questioned. Commitment to religious authority is replaced by defining religion as an expression of the popular will. Populism of all sorts seems a logical response of a generation alienated from major institutions of the society. Thus the incorporation of this age group into the religious institution may already have stimulated some of the populist expressions mentioned above. Since they are now young adults and are a particularly numerous cohort, it is likely that such trends will continue in the churches for some time to come.

A Look at the Younger Cohort

However, in discussing the uniqueness of this age cohort, we must also test its experience against that of younger age groups. Can we see the Vietnam generation as the first of a new wave that will extend into the future for an indeterminate time? Are trends begun by this age group likely to be congruent with the styles and needs of the next group of young people to take their place, or has this been a unique cohort in the sense of being out of phase with both those older and those younger in the society?

Trends that affected the experience and response of the Vietnam generation are still a part of the environment, not only in America but also worldwide, at least in those societies that might be characterized as postmodern, past the early stages of economic development. In a study of nine European nations as well as the United States, Inglehart divided respondents into "Materialist" and "Post-Materialist" categories along lines similar to Yankelovich's "career-minded" and "post-affluent" groups mentioned earlier. He found a growing percentage of "Post-Materialists" in all the societies studied, particularly among young college-educated people—the same segment of the population that was most affected by the counterculture. According to Inglehart, the responses of the "Post-Materialist" were stimulated by five significant changes in Western society: (1) a great increase in higher education; (2) a great increase in intercultural communication through mass media and international travel; (3) technological changes that have brought about a higher standard of living; (4) changes in the occupational structure, particularly with a rise in sectors not directly related to production; and (5) increased employment outside the home for women.[13] All these have affected young people, and there is no reason to think that they will not continue to have a similar effect in the future.

On this basis, we should expect to find younger age groups accepting the responses of the dominant style of the late 1960s and early 1970s, which we have tied to such changes in the society. But there is little evidence of this kind. Acceptance by younger age groups of countercultural styles has been very selective, and the selection has been of those elements often furthest removed from the primary ideological focus of the counterculture. Instead of seeking to create a new culture, most younger people find countercultural styles attractive only if they can enhance their personal lives or help them to escape any social responsibility. There is little in this younger age cohort to make the observer believe that the ideals of the counterculture have been passed on by their originators to a new generation that is carrying them on. In fact, just the opposite seems to be the case. Rather than continuing the revolt against the life-style of the postwar period, youth of the early 1980s seem eager to participate in a nostalgia craze that celebrates that very period. The way many of today's youth speak of the generation slightly older than they are does not reflect emulation or appreciation so much as a general sense of disapproval. Not only do the upheavals of the Vietnam period appear to have been a short-term aberration in the American historical process, but they seem also to have created their own rebels in the younger brothers and sisters who follow after the Vietnam generation. If the older youth were suffering from social dislocation, it may be said that the younger ones are part of a second wave of dislocation which has set up unique reactions in this new generation.

We have said that one of the common experiences in the formative years of the Vietnam generation was that of pressure from social forces that seemed alien, appearing to push young people into life-styles and identities that they found alien. Their reaction to such experiences, however, created a very different environment for the next younger age cohort. By the time these young people reached high school and college, the educational system had responded significantly to its critics. Standardized programs of study had been blown apart, giving way to greater freedom of choice by students as to what courses they might take. Grading systems in many schools had been abolished, replaced by simple designations of "pass/fail" or "credit/no credit." Classrooms had been democratized; the authority of teachers was questioned by students, by community members from outside the school, by governmental regulators. Civil rights activism had created school populations that represented a wide range of subcultures and life-styles—so wide a range that students sometimes found it hard to communicate with one another. Teachers, often poorly prepared for so much diversity in the classroom and grappling with a slipping authority, often found it impossible to do much more than keep order. Many students, in consequence, found the school to be a place of chaos, disorder, and confusion.

In the family as well, older brothers and sisters or neighbors had created havoc in traditional relationships, declaring their independence, scorning the life-style of their parents, calling into question not only their authority but also their virtue. For many in the younger cohort, these conditions became very specific and personally harmful, undermining the verities of their childish social world. Later they may have also discovered that their families had used up funds set aside for their education to attempt to rescue older siblings from foreign or domestic jails or to put them through drug rehabilitation programs or the like.

Their perception of public events was also very different from that of the older group. In a group of college freshmen in 1978, several said that their earliest memory of TV news was of John Kennedy's funeral. They were only about three years old at the time, but they remembered the drums, the horses, and the vague sense of sadness and loss, of something very wrong. After that, and clear in the memory of all these young people, came riots in the streets, burning cities, the assassinations of Martin Luther King, Jr., and Robert Kennedy, all those months of Vietnam news footage, and then Watergate. For these young people the problem was not dealing with demands for conformity to the "system"; it was finding any kind of system at all that might help them to define their lives.

Some members of the older, parental generation may have idealized the cause of countercultural rebels. This younger generation saw little about the rebellion that was idealistic. In their experience it was self-serving activity of the worst sort, shallow, childish, and vain. Yet there was one thing that they shared with the older cohort. Like them, this younger group found themselves cut off from the mainstream of the society and its institutions. The normal patterns of gaining one's identity in a fairly fixed and bounded group and then, perhaps, outgrowing it had been destroyed, as those secure groups had been dissolved. So this age cohort, too, was set on a path seeking personal identity, the haunting journey in search of the self. This time, however, there was no reason to assume that the self must be found by breaking out of any social bonds. Rather, many in the younger cohort sought selfhood and identity in community—not the fluid and fully voluntary communities of the counterculture, but authoritarian, closed communities that could ward off chaos and assure one of structure and purpose.

Populism, religious or otherwise, has a very different cast among people who are, in their own minds, seeking to exercise free choice of social alternatives than among those who are desperately seeking something to hang onto in a situation that appears chaotic. Among the former there tends to be an element of playfulness, a willingness to hold one's options open. If a populist situation has indeed produced organizations that treat people as a mass audience or market, the attitude of the people is more like that of the market where buyers pick and choose, weigh costs and bargain. By contrast, among those who are seeking a way out of chaos, the response is more likely to be that of the mob, swayed by a leader to make emotional commitments to ill-considered action.

Perhaps the boundaries of the Vietnam generation as the more open populist type were reached in the political movements with the accession to leadership of those grim revolutionaries who could give no quarter. There is a great gap between those who chose to stick flowers in the rifle barrels of National Guard troops sent to keep them in line and the closed violence of, for example, the Symbionese Liberation Army in its later stages. In religion, the shift could be seen in the move from open groups to secret ones that demanded total commitment of adherents. Sometimes the transformation has occurred in an entire group, as has been documented, for example, in some Jesus Movement groups[14] as well as in the Church of Scientology.[15] The process has been shown to be a response to the needs of leaders to retain authority and of members who want authoritative structure to their lives.

Methods of Reentry into the Mainstream

In all this—and many other examples could be given—we find evidence of the uniqueness of the age cohort that comprised the postwar baby boom and the youth of the Vietnam era. Their formative experiences have set them off from both older and younger cohorts to the extent that genuine understanding across age lines is difficult. Some of their number opted out of the social process during their youthful years and remain outside, isolated in rural or urban communes or continuing to drift from place to place or group to group without settling in any one. Most, however, either experienced those formative years in ways that did not pull them all the way out of the social order or have been reabsorbed into it. They are now, themselves, in the once-alien category of "over thirty." But to paraphrase Jess Moody's comment quoted previously, there is no way that they can be over thirty the way people before them were over thirty. They carry with them into later life the experiences of their youth. They are, if you will, "branded" by those experiences.

They are also very numerous. And since they are both numerous and unique, they continue to engage the interest of intellectuals and the media. Their interests continue to seem to be the *Zeitgeist*. It is no coincidence that streets depicted in the media, once full of rioters, are now full of joggers. The passion for physical fitness now animating these people moving out of youth's careless acceptance of health and strength has infected the entire population. New forms of populist alienation from social institutions may be found in movements in defense of ecological balance and opposing nuclear power, but far more notably in consumer movements. It is also evident in the orientation of many people to the institutions they now have entered, as can be seen in listings of recent best-selling nonfiction: *Winning Through Intimidation, Looking Out for Number 1,* and the like. For many, reentry has been accompanied by some sense of defeat and cynicism, a notion that "if you can't fight them, join them," but also that institutions may be used to one's own ends. This kind of cynicism can be particularly infectious among younger people who were never inspired to fight against social forces and may be easily persuaded to a kind of isolated individualism willing to use any and all occasions for personal gain. Personal identity not really fully achieved becomes the object of restless acquisition, seeking expansion as a substitute for definition.

It must be said that such cynical and selfish reentry into society does not characterize the entire age cohort, even if it seems at times to be the dominant mode by far. There is another mode of reentry that has been the style of some of these people that may bear with it far more lasting influences for social and cultural change. These are the people who have never given up the more idealistic aspects of the cultural rebellion, who have found places in the society in which they can act out those ideals. They may be seen as something approaching a cultural fifth column, living proof that there are other values and other world views that one may live by in contrast to the dominant culture.

Many live quiet, somewhat lonely lives, usually working in service professions, sometimes at very low pay, declaring by their actions a devotion to human values beyond the materialism of the culture. They work among the poor, the aged, or the outcast, quietly helping to ameliorate some of the more galling aspects of existence for their clients. Others, who may not have given up on the social order quite as much, engage in such activities but also continue to put pressure on the social system to effect changes, working through the agencies they serve or the voluntary groups of which they are a part. They are found in centers offering inexpensive legal services, health clinics, schools, welfare agencies, and the like. Others, often living in religious communities of some sort, still seek to organize opposition to things they see as particularly glaring social ills.

In overview, then, the adaptation of the Vietnam generation to society seems to have taken two very distinct directions. One is a cynical giving in to the "system" while retaining the right to use it for one's selfish ends. The other is an extension of earlier methods of nonviolent resistence, where one may appear to conform but directs one's actions toward ends and values not evident in the usual understanding of the system. The result of either of these forms of participation, particularly if engaged in by a significant proportion of this populous age cohort, can be revolutionary. Constant turning of social activity to private ends that are not consistent with the public good can create the conditions of social collapse. Dedicating social activity to new goals and values may in the long run not fully collapse the society, but it may so alter it as to change the culture radically.

It would seem, then, that the quiet rebels are the ones most fully living up to the mandate given their generation to usher in a new age. However, their numbers and influence, at least at the present time, do not seem sufficient to effect that change. We have been, of course, throughout this discussion speaking once again of the most visible adaptations. Even added together, the numbers fully immersed in either of the styles just mentioned could hardly claim a majority of this age cohort. The people in between, most probably never having been totally immersed in the counterculture or in reaction against it, yet affected by it as one of the factors impinging on their identity as it was being formed, remain the pool from which one or the other response may draw recruits. Unless they have lived in situations insulated from the public media, these young adults have heard too much criticism of the society to fall back into comfortable, unexamined acceptance of the status quo. If their lives reflect the status quo, they are likely to suffer occasional pangs of conscience about it or to defend their position with excessive vigor. If the "quiet rebels" can capture their imaginations, the process of social change may be accelerated in the direction envisioned by early celebrators of the counterculture. If not, defensive reaction may win their allegiance. The polarization represented by those who might be called the "selfish" and the "selfless" adaptors is likely to be found in other types of movements agitating this age group, all more extreme than might appeal to persons whose early experiences had been more consistent and positive.

Consequences of the Counterculture

In the meantime, the movements and responses among this age group are setting up the conditions under which the next cohort are coming of age. Definitions of the place of youth in the society have come to be based on the experiences of the Vietnam generation, taking for granted the opposition that developed in a generation battling for some kind of relief from the oppressive forces of the society of their day as they perceived them. What faces many people in the younger cohort is less a negative contact with the rest of the society than no contact at all. The countercultural years have speeded up a process already begun in which the society seems to have behaved like many organisms which deal with internal, existence-threatening irritations by walling them off. The affluence of American society has allowed us to surround our young with a dazzling array of gadgets, entertainments, and activities. We may find that those things are the equivalent of the pearl produced by the oyster to reduce friction from a grain of sand—beautiful, less irritating, but totally encasing and imprisoning the sand. Assumptions about youth, reinforced by those whose experience of it was made painful by a restrictive society, have set up the conditions under which it is difficult for the young to find any channels for responsible participation in the society as a whole.

This is not immediately apparent; on the surface just the opposite has been the case. It was due to pressure from youthful dissidents during the Vietnam period that the voting age was lowered from twenty-one to eighteen, and with it many other restrictions removed from younger citizens. It was out of the same era that students came to be included on many boards and committees of schools and universities, and youth representatives were made part of many decision-making bodies of other voluntary and public organizations. People who fought hard to open such pathways to participation have expressed deep disappointment with the low level of participation by today's young, but their response may simply reflect the effectiveness of informal social forces working against such participation. So many assumptions about the uniqueness of the youth culture reinforce a sense of isolation in their own age group that it becomes hard for the young to find participation in adult institutions relevant to their lives. There is little reward in the peer group for the young person who puts in long, hard hours on adult committees. The products of those committees, the plans and projects of adult organizations, are not generally things that concern the young, who are expected to spend their time and energy on activities limited to their age group—recreation, sports, their own distinctive music, expressive activities, "making it" in school or in social life. The purpose of life for the young seems to be defined primarily as the pursuit of happiness, most often through the use of all the products and techniques developed and marketed through the society for that purpose. Unable yet to relate to the means of production that require specialized technical expertise, not expected to have any stake in the society except in keeping its pressures at bay, they have become the primary consumers of a consumption-oriented society. Media programs oriented to the young consumer get top ratings and bring the top dollar from advertisers. Responsible participation in the society has been traded for irresponsible enjoyment of its products.

How could this be the consequence of a generation that rebelled against the shallowness of a consumer society? Certainly it was not intended. Yet the emphasis on feeling and celebration in the counterculture was one happily picked up by the entertainment industry to be exploited in a great variety of ways, and it was through this industry rather than through ideological statements that most of the younger generation heard about the movements that preceded them. This interpretation of the movement, while seldom a conscious plot, may well have seemed not too bad an idea to older members of the society after they had learned the potential of ideologically motivated youth for disruption and violence. It was easy to encourage such apparently harmless diversions. The problem may be that they are not only temporary diversions but also serious detours on the path to social maturity. Involvement in adult society has, in most societies, been a progressive, cumulative process, with the youth gradually assuming more and more responsibility, first for one's self, then for others. One of the consequences of the counterculture seems to have been the creation of a gap between personal and social responsibility, or at least a weakening of any sense of obligation to those outside one's particular group. The ways in which the young are initiated into a wider consciousness of kind appear to have been eroded, as the young adults ahead of them in the process seem to have broken a number of bridges to that consciousness.

At the same time, that generation of young adults who came of age during the Vietnam period still seems isolated from older groups, pushing into adulthood without identifying with others who occupy that social category. Their ambivalence toward identifying with society as a whole is becoming less attached to age as an identifying symbol and more to particular issues they find important. As a result, the political process has been invaded by a type of politics where votes are cast on the basis of a candidate's stand on just one issue, regardless of the consequences of his or her stand on any other subject.

Single-issue politics are contagious in that they engender countermovements equally focused on the particular stance that is being pushed. The polarization endemic in the Vietnam generation is pushing the society not just toward equal polarization but to a potential shattering into political fragments with little vested interest in any group's interests but their own. This undermines the very basis of American politics, where compromise and concession have always been undertaken in the name of the larger good, so that even small minorities have been able to have some influence because of interests that overlap.

Thus the age cohort we have called the Vietnam generation is unique in its relations with the rest of the adult world of which it has become a part. There is less commitment in this age cohort to social and political styles previously taken for granted as setting the ground rules for resolving differences and accomplishing the public good. Because of its size and its position at a break in social consciousness, this cohort appears to be particularly influential. It has proven its ability to disrupt the social process. What remains to be seen is whether these young adults can also provide the genesis of social reconstruction which was the mandate given them—without their full consent—by a society still unsure of its future direction.

Chapter 5

Religion, the Church, and Modern Society

It may be useful at this point to review some of the ways in which the church has been involved in the shaping of the cohort of young adults who came of age during the Vietnam period. We seem to have found in this age group a muddled ambivalence toward religion, sometimes scorning it entirely, sometimes demanding the right to behave in a manner more explicitly religious than has been encouraged by most mainline churches, sometimes demanding new models and expressions not related to the common religious base of the culture. We look for common patterns in the experience of this generation in the society's religious institutions and in the response of the churches to the movements that arose during the activist years.

The search begins in the years in which were established the families that were to nurture a generation of postwar children. We have traced patterns of migration and social mobility that characterized the society immediately after World War II and some of the ways in which the churches were used in the process of culture building by a generation that had been thoroughly uprooted. The roots of ambivalence toward religion in the Vietnam generation may be traced to patterns impinging on their families, as changes in religious styles were among the many social processes that took a quantum leap during that period. For that significant portion of the population that were the first of their family to attend college, thanks to the GI Bill, the change in point of view and in social status that accompanied their education implied a drastic change in religious style. The blue-collar families in which they had grown up were, for the most part, involved in a religious style that emphasized personal piety, moral rectitude, and simple expressions of religious feeling. Their attachment to the church tended to depend upon local neighborhood ties. With a college education that removed them far from the neighborhood, many of the returned GIs were weaned away from this kind of natural and communal piety. For many, the secular humanism of the universities was both liberating and more sensible, and so they simply dropped their church participation in a process of erosion that has long been associated with higher education. But there were too many veterans on campus, too many students crowding classrooms and campus activities for all to find a real community in the "community of scholars"; and their war-nourished longings for home and neighborhood dictated a return to communal roots that had been expressed in the churches of their youth. So they flocked to the newly built suburban churches, finding many that were not in opposition to the secular humanism of the university, that were trying to build new communities among the uprooted through their varied activities, expressing the new kind of homogeneity found in the suburbs. The integration of styles represented in these churches was a rather loose amalgam of the personal piety of the roots of many of their members and the yearning for cosmopolitan, heterogeneous sociability that reflected a new and more diverse social experience. They were, in this latter context, more likely to deal with elements of public piety than the working class churches from which many of their members had come, but their concept of the public piety still had a tribal tinge.

The nature of public piety in the postwar years was largely shaped by public events of the period, particularly the cold war, so that one common aspect among the many churches was that celebration of the American way of life that came to be known as American civil religion. Will Herberg's *Protestant-Catholic-Jew* documented the way in which once-ethnic churches had become primarily organizations devoted to the celebration of the American way of life in the slightly differing styles of the three major faiths of the title.[1] Churchgoing came to be, in part, an expression of patriotism—often of national chauvinism. If the founders of the country had indeed dreamed of establishing a New Israel on these virgin shores, it seemed that God had shown approval by blessing the nation with vast material and cultural wealth, elevating it to world status as a superpower. The problem, of course, was that the other superpower able to contest our status was the Soviet Union, a nation whose Marxist/Communist creed rejected religion and so deserved no such blessing from a righteous God. In the secular segment of American society, as well as in the churches, contrasts were made between "godless communism" and "Christian capitalism." In those days, churchgoing clearly put one on the side of the angels in the international context, and refusing to be identified with one of the three major Western branches of the Judeo-Christian tradition made one's patriotism and reliability suspect.

In some of those churches there was some ambivalence about being the instrument of national pride. The "suburban captivity" of the churches was not only expressed in life-style but also in an assumed politics that some church leaders found suspect. For some of the children growing up in these churches there was great disparity in what they perceived as the reasons they were sent to church school and what they learned there. The conflict between the two led some to find in the churches a clear example of the hypocrisy of adult society. For most, however, the conflict was not that evident. It was simply clear to them that the churches were part of the institutional structure of the society that was demanding of them a kind of cultural conformity as the operative statement of their faith. Frequently, for those not brought up in the church it seemed even more clear that the churches were agents of the "system."

The Churches and the Transformation of Society

For most countercultural rebels, the churches were clearly a part of the culture which must be overturned. If the churches represented the political pole opposite "godless communism" (and that kind of bipolar thinking had led to the Vietnam debacle that threatened the lives of this age cohort in particular), then the churches were the enemy. If the churches nourished the suburban families that now were being blamed for pushing a shallow conformity on their children, then the churches were a despised wedge between youth and those they would have liked to have loved and to have been loved by in return. In school, young people studied about the Protestant Ethic and, assuming it still to be operative, blamed the churches for pushing the kind of social and economic mobility that had left their families—and themselves—rootless and shallow.

Yet the churches themselves offered no such monolithic stance toward the culture. It was hard for suburban congregations to resist the cultural models since they were the apparent basis of their success. People joined in order to express their acceptance of the social order. They enrolled their children in the bulging religious classrooms so that they would learn to be good citizens—honest, moral, and dependable. They pledged money to building funds, knowing that thriving church plants in a neighborhood increased property values and might enrich the quality of life. They gave money to church benevolent causes as proof that Americans were good people, kindly and generous.

There could also be found in the suburban churches as elsewhere another facet of Christianity—and of Judaism. It was, however, more common in specialized ministries less impacted by a clientele seeking cultural conformity. Citing the tradition of the prophets, these church people refused to propagate a doctrine of "Christ of culture," as H. R. Niebuhr defined it, choosing instead to point to "Christ as the transformer of culture."[2] They assumed that the religious tradition, grounded in a God beyond any human culture, should provide a base for cultural criticism. Religious visions of the kingdom of God have always been more perfect than any human society, but at least in the minds of these "transformationists" such visions stand as models toward which any society should strive and by which it should be evaluated. They demanded a more universal model for individual and corporate morality than that of American society. In looking at American culture, they could see room for improvement, and they called for it in the name of God.

Perhaps the finest hour of those who sought to transform the culture through religion came at the very beginning of the activist years, in the civil rights struggle. The figure of Martin Luther King, Jr., looms high in their midst. Here a young black minister, not at all eager to leave the security of a congregation more culturally affirming than many black churches, was thrust into leadership of a movement distinguished from culture-bound definitions both in its vision and in its methods. While Americans have long given lip service to equality and brotherhood, in actual practice the society has always recognized cultural and social distinctions between the races. Much of the lip service given a more universal view of humanity had occurred in the churches, but there was little evidence of it in their practice, where, as it was frequently observed, the traditional hour of Sunday morning worship was the most segregated hour of the week. King, often speaking within the context of American civil religion, offered a compelling vision of a more perfect society: "I have a dream. . . ." The method of nonviolent resistance violated all cultural norms. Not only was it deviant to break laws, no matter how unjust; but also it was even more deviant to do so in ways guaranteed to evoke punishment and not to retaliate in kind. King quite properly expressed impatience with other Christians and Jews for their lack of support for the movement; however, there were a considerable number who responded to the call, participated in demonstrations and freedom rides, marched and sang and prayed together, in a compelling experience of religious unity; clergy and laity, Catholic, Protestant, and Jew, black and white, young and old, linked arms and offered a visible alternative to the structures and divisions of the society, led by this black clergyman, all within the framework of a religiously grounded vision of human society as God intended it.

Not many of the Vietnam age cohort were old enough to participate in this movement. These earlier recruits were less totally alienated from the social system, more hopeful that it could be reformed by their actions. They did in the long run effect a good deal of change, but it could hardly be said that they transformed the society. Even the changes that were made were often accomplished in ways that turned positive gains into problems. So while many church people remember their days of participation in the civil rights movement as high points of their careers, as an experience of the reality of alternate models of human society that are far more satisfying than the current order, younger people who could only observe results found little to celebrate. King was dead, the victim of an assassin's bullet; so much for the willingness of the society to be reformed by that movement. And all those people of goodwill seemed to have gone home to their former pursuits, leaving the people they had tried to help to struggle with the consequences of institutional racism, albeit in different forms. The primary legacy given to the Vietnam generation was not faith in the vision of a better society founded in the religion of the nation or a demonstration of the effectiveness of nonviolent resistance as both disrupting the present order and modeling a better one, but proof that powerless people can disrupt things with mass demonstrations and in the process can make their complaints heard by attracting media attention. The more positive and religious aspects were lost in the perception of a generation already convinced that the society wished them not good but evil. The lessons that were learned were those that could be used to express their alienation.

A constant problem for many church people who continued to hope for a transformation of the society based on religious visions of the kingdom of God, who hoped that the counterculture might be a vehicle of transformation, was the rejection of the religious vision by those whose alienation from the society included among their enemies the churches. This was the dilemma of many campus ministers, who seemed to be pushed into making a choice between the churches and the young people they served in the name of those churches. Caught in the middle, they often angered both constituencies because they would not choose between them. Or else they did choose and, in so doing, lost entirely their contact with the side chosen against. Either way, alienation from the church was not ameliorated. Defectors to the counterculture proved the point that the churches were unworthy of the loyalty of the young. Defectors from the young proved to their generation that church people were unreliable, enemy agents in their midst. Staying on the fence proved that the church had no stomach for the commitments required in the building of a new age and so could be safely ignored. It was a no-win situation.

    Yet we have seen how religious the counterculture was in its unique fashion. Forms of experiential religion, recovery of ancient forms, crosscultural borrowing of religious styles—all came to a focus in the counterculture. Another dimension, less noticeable, was the ethical fallout of some of the transformational religion, separated from its church base by the generation's rejection of religious and other social institutions. Whatever such movements as that for civil rights may have accomplished in changing the society, they reinforced some of the ideals of more secular celebrators of the counterculture and quickened consciences of many members of the Vietnam generation. There remain in that age group many inheritors of the spirit of the Peace Corps and Vista volunteers, the civil rights activists, and other reformers. Their problem has been the breakdown of institutional channels they can trust as instruments of their idealism.

The Churches and the New Life-Styles

The Vietnam generation has now passed into young adulthood, but their unique experience has resulted in somewhat different patterns of entry into that status. This has particular relevance for the churches. For example, a common pattern of religious commitment has been for young people to drift away from active congregational involvement, to return after marriage and particularly after having children, for whom they look to the church to provide basic religious education and a supportive community. One of the alterations in the common pattern found in the Vietnam generation came out of their alienation from the institution of the family. They tended, first of all, to postpone marriage. Suspicious of long-term commitments that might force them into lives that would cramp their newfound—or still avidly sought—identities, they chose instead to exercise the sexual freedom proclaimed by the counterculture. They lived together as couples without marital commitments, or as mixed groups, or in homosexual liaisons. Or they kept free of all involvements, drifting from place to place, from person to person, moving on whenever they felt threatened by a growing sense of obligation to anyone. Children presented many problems. First, of course, they did imply those lasting obligations that could impair the sacred pursuit of personal identity. Second, it seemed to many of these young people that it would be cruel to bring children into such a hostile world. The general apocalyptic mood contributed to such an evaluation; an investment in the future—which children are—is inappropriate among those who perceive themselves to be at the end of an age, with the future a real question. And, of course, one of the apocalyptic visions was that of a world overpopulated and overcrowded, inspiring among these young people movements for zero population growth and more reason not to establish families.

All this has created problems for churches which have long functioned on a model that takes the nuclear family as the basic unit of the congregation. They have had a tendency to acquiesce to the pattern that assumes temporary defection of youth while they work through the process of gaining an adult identity over against such units of childhood formation as the family and the local church. At best, they hoped to keep them in contact with the church through youth groups and campus ministries only tenuously related to the central programs of a congregation. As many of those ministries broke down following the activist period, there were few channels of involvement for those who would act out adult commitment in social service through the church or even would try to expand their horizons of thought beyond the local community. Few local congregations have provided activities for adults who are unmarried, and church teachings have not given much aid and comfort to those living together without benefit of clergy, even less if the liaisons are homosexual rather than heterosexual. So as the period of separation from nuclear family units has grown in length, the loss of contact between the churches and this age cohort has become an apparently permanent pattern. There has been a tendency in recent years for many of these young adults to return to patterns of marriage and child rearing, though at a later age. It may be hard for them now to break long-standing habits that made no place in their lives for church participation or in their meaning systems for the use of religious language for interpreting their actions.

There are also other barriers to the pattern of easy return. In the politics of the Vietnam war, many church people continued to reflect the national chauvinism of the civil religion of the 1950s even though others—particularly church professionals outside the congregational structure—were deeply involved in antiwar movements out of their religious convictions. The experience of many young people in local congregations did not give them assurance of a warm welcome should they return to church still holding a political view that had been unpopular.

A particularly important factor is the lack of fit in patterns of living between this generation and most church congregations. While young adults have, for the most part, returned to the economic system to do the kinds of work ordinarily expected of people with their background and training, their alienation may be seen in attitudes toward work. There are few in this age group who resonate to the world view of the so-called Protestant Ethic, who find fulfillment and self-expression in their work. Those who do find such satisfaction tend to be the ones who have opted for lives at the margin of the economy, who make a minimal living through handicrafts or similar personal endeavors. For many, economic marginality has also implied remaining on the margin of social institutions such as the church. Most of those that are at work in the mainstream of the economy simply do the work required of them as something necessary to provide the funds for activities that are the real focus of their lives—primarily forms of recreation. This means, among other things, that weekends are likely to be spent away from home, or Saturday night celebrations are likely to presuppose a Sunday to sleep late and be quiet. Such a life-style has little relevance to a pattern of church programming focused on Sunday morning. Returning to active involvement in the church may mean for many of today's young adults a major reversal of their style of life—small wonder that the churches most successful in inducing that return have been those that stress a conversion experience!

It is of particular importance to the churches that the influence of this large cohort of young adults has spread to much of the rest of the society, particularly their attitude toward work and leisure, for it seems to fly in the face of an ethic traditionally honored by the churches, at least in this country. The contrast may be shown in the following quote by Horace Sutton from a recent *Saturday Review* article on travel in the 1980s:

> Most of us had grown up with a sense of self-denial. . . . Spending money on one's self was against the ethic of the time. One's job and one's home were the important aspects of one's life, and travel played a marginal role. But new values were born in the Sixties and they spread in the Seventies to the rest of the population. We shifted away from self-denial and began to enrich ourselves by expanding our horizons. Travel has ceased to be marginal. It is no longer a luxury, but part of a life plan. We may need to make some cutbacks—pare a three-week trip to a fortnight, a winter's week in the sun or the snow to a long weekend. Those are but economic

adjustments. There is an accepted need to escape, a right to escape in the face of stress. The shift from self-denial to spending on oneself may well be what life will be all about for that dauntless dasher, the 80s Traveler.[3]

In essence, the life-style described here rejects the "inner-worldly asceticism" that Max Weber found characteristic of Protestantism in particular. There is evidence that some churches, at least, are willing also to reject such a world view, though they may not have deliberately set out to do so. It is apparent in the offerings of some of the more popular forms of religion of our time that this need to escape, to enjoy time off, has come to be accepted and catered to. Beginning with the "electronic church," which inhabits the entertainment media and often has the polished style of show business, we may also move out to observe congregations whose worship services offer colorful pageantry, messages not far removed from commercial "hype," music that has the flair of the stage. These tend to be the churches that are growing. These have responded to the religious populism of the time, and people are likely to shop around for religious services as they do for other kinds of weekend entertainment. Those "shoppers" do not just represent the young adults in the age group we have been discussing, though they may have been influenced by them. This is a widespread phenomenon, a pattern of the "Christ of culture" that reveals the extent to which modern definitions of worth have been influenced by such devices as television's ratings system and other popularity polls.

All too often the main-line churches, in contrast to populist movements, have given the appearance of representing the elites and elite intellectuals that populism decries. They have fallen into another way of mirroring the culture, this time that part of it that composes the "new class" of people whose work is with ideas and information. Based firmly in the secular humanism of the academic background of this class, these churches may offer programs less in the genre of show business than that of popular psychological movements. They pick up the countercultural emphases on personal involvement, self-discovery, expressing one's feelings, and the like, to form small groups whose aim is personal fulfillment. They may well also affirm elements of "high culture" in sophisticated aesthetic expression in their rituals and music. The contrast between these churches and the more populist types indicates ways in which the churches themselves mirror the polarizations within the culture rather than offering a unitary view of the Christian hope for humankind.

Against both these forms of Christianity, yet still within the tradition, are the direct inheritors of some of the political movements of the counterculture. These groups, in the tradition of the early Anabaptist sects, proclaim a clearly delineated stance that puts them in direct opposition to the culture. They reflect the opposition in their life-style, where they live simply, often communally, rejecting all the blandishments of a consumer society. Their politics flow directly from the counterculture's opposition to "big government," and they stand also in opposition to most of the economic policies of the society, are ardently pacifist, and are advocates for the poor and those suffering from violations of human rights in this country as well as outside it. As they oppose the centralized systems of the society, these groups stand politically as the most populist of all. Yet their opposition to the "popular will" tends to insert one more element of disunity into the religious picture.

Populism has had—and deserved—a respected place in the history of American society. As a reflection of the popular will made evident in specific movements, it has forced power holders of the society to be more sensitive to a wider constituency. As a protest movement, populism has called to account many aspects of the society that may have been developing in directions unacceptable to the majority, possibly even unintended by those responsible for them. Populism in American churches has kept them from being priest-ridden or irrelevant, pulling the teeth of anticlerical movements or cynical acceptance of religion as a tool of the establishment.

However, populism works best in a dialectical process, as a movement against certain abuses that may result in reform but not in a complete takeover by the movement. Popular movements are commonly based on a few specific issues rather than a total vision of the way things should be ordered. Few people can stand firmly in the grassroots and see all of the "big picture." In religious institutions in particular, where there is an assumption that some vision of the kingdom underlies the interests and causes of the present, it is never enough to have the churches reflect the will of the people. There is an underlying expectation of religious institutions that they will assist people in reaching beyond their current sensibilities and understandings. Populist rebellions in the church may properly question the direction in which the people are being led, but they lose their religious charter if they assume that the only duty of the churches is to affirm opinions where they currently stand.

Reintegrating the Dislocated

Troeltsch, in his massive recapitulation of the ways in which the Christian churches have through time related to the societies in which they have been found, has pointed up a peculiar strength of the medieval Catholic church, which incorporated its sectarian movements into the larger organization, making of them special orders, each with its own charter.[4] Since the Protestant Reformation, sectarian movements have tended to keep their own separate organizations, and yet in America the acceptance of the plural model of a denominational society has amounted to an informal co-optation of sectarian movements into the religious institution of the nation. Sects—the churches of the disinherited—have in the long run helped their people to an appropriation of their inheritance as members of the society.

The religious populism of the Vietnam generation may be the expression of another kind of disinheritance, where the young were pushed forward toward the future by an older generation that was too unsure of itself to lead them, where there were all too few visionaries from the churches equal to the task of equipping them for the journey, much less of accompanying them. Those most willing to involve themselves with youth who tried to create a new culture tended to be the least supportive of—or supported by—the churches. The need for sectarian religion could be expected to arise.

Religious movements, of course, are not the only possibility in this situation. They would probably not have been the recourse at this time if there had been other social institutions in which this generation's push to the future could have been supported. For several generations the colleges and universities had served this purpose for many, but now they were severely divided and distraught. To many of the young they were simply one more organ of a repressive system, all the more repellent because of their familiarity. Graduate students and some faculty, supported by a few administrators, had attempted to institute changes of all kinds—new courses, new majors, new grading systems, new admissions policies, new administrative and decision-making systems, new forms of supervision for student housing and student life. Already overburdened by too rapid growth, academic organizations creaked, shuddered, and threatened to break down. They were hardly in a position to nurture the movement toward cultural innovation which they had helped to midwife. It was no time, either, to look to the political institution for steady assistance. Even if it had not become a primary enemy during Vietnam, the final blows given the system by Watergate ensured that it would not be easy to find resources there for the construction of a new order.

In other words, the final understanding of this as a "dislocated" generation has to come from the loss of any clear routes into the social order as it is now or as it might become. There remains a conviction that there is a basic need for change, for reordering, for dealing with the processes and systems of the society in some way. The conditions of society are still present that led older generations to pin their hopes for the future on the first generation to have as their birthright the cultural realities of post-World War II civilization. The particular response that came to be known as the counterculture has dissipated without effecting the changes that its apostles expected of it. But the problem of finding appropriate cultural adjustments to a future dominated by modern technology and rapid change remains a necessity. The task of cultural reconstruction was inappropriately laid on the shoulders of a single age cohort, but as adults in today's society they can hardly escape bearing part of the burden. It is essential that pathways to responsible participation in the society be opened and strengthened for this cohort as well as for those who follow after them and have also suffered dislocation because of disruptions in the process of social integration of the young. The search for identity must not only deal with the internal dimensions of the self or relatedness in some small group but also with an exploration of the public aspects of the person—concepts poorly developed in the lives of today's youth and young adults.

The definition of democracy in this nation that has caught the moral imagination of humankind is that of a general and responsible participation in the public process. The many movements of the recent and historic past, as well as the present, can be described as attempts of groups previously left out to enter into that kind of participation. Blacks, ethnic minorities, youth, women, others whose style of life has been treated as a disqualification for participation, have been the protagonists in the past couple of decades. *Access* to the process has in many cases been achieved, but that is only part of what is required. It must be complemented by the development of skills and points of view that make it possible for persons to identify with the public process as participants, to seek the public good as an extension of private interest rather than as something exterior and potentially inimical to the individual.

Social critics properly point out that this process has always been imperfect and has been particularly ineffective in recent years. But there have been recognized patterns, channels through which the formation of a public identity has been achieved. For people already in the mainstream, educational institutions, public and private, have complemented the teaching of families about the nature of public morality for persons in their particular niche in society. The nature of the workplace has dictated some of the specifics of that morality, with a greater emphasis on personal behavior for those at the lower rungs of the ladder and on community responsibility for those whose actions and decisions have direct consequences in the lives of others. But there has also been an assumption that one may move from the one place, from the one morality, to another. Americans have been particularly understanding of the parable of the good steward: "You have been faithful over a little, I will set you over much . . ." (Matthew 25:23). The churches, by and large, have helped with the formation of moral character by reinforcing the same models, according to the dominant social characteristics of their members and their aspirations. The mechanics for getting into the system were also often the province of religious groups, as various sects set standards of behavior as evidence of sanctification that resulted in the development of a pattern of reliability and responsibility. Such styles of life tended to open doors to occupations that allowed a family to enter the economic and social mainstream where the other social institutions could function effectively for them. In recent years we have depended upon social welfare programs to provide this function; but since they have little access to the roots of motivation the way religious groups can have, they have generally been less effective.

The question now at hand, however, is no longer only that of providing access to the system for those kept out by poverty and lack of economic skills. Rather we are faced with a generation that has lost fruitful contact with the institutions of the society because of the speed of upward mobility of their families. The kinds of morality taught in their childhood have become inappropriate in a new age with a choice of new lifestyles and a new set of responsibilities. The notion of public responsibility at a level commensurate with their current status has not taken root. Where are the mechanisms of the formation of public character by which these dislocated people may be brought into the processes by which the society is maintained and renewed? Are new religious groups of our day a potential source of reintegration, as historic sects have been? Have main-line religious denominations any stake in the process?

Religion and Social Integration

There is strong evidence that the Jesus Movement of recent decades provided a route from the counterculture back into that portion of mainstream society represented by evangelical churches, the most direct inheritors of historic sects. There is some doubt, however, as to whether those churches, in their current affirmation of most of the elements of the culture, define salvation in such a way as to have social significance. For many, being born again carries little notion of a change of behavior in ways that affect the society at large. We now see evidence that some young adults in that tradition are beginning to feel the need for broader applications of their faith. Alumni of the Jesus Movement are now applying to the more liberal seminaries, seeking ways of putting to work the religious convictions formed in their passage in the reconstruction of the culture that was part of the legacy of their generation. Dissatisfied with the easy affirmation of the culture and the individualistic emphases in many of the evangelical churches, they seek the roots of Christian reform among churches that are the inheritors of the social gospel, while still holding to a theology that allows them to affirm transcendent legitimation for their efforts. They challenge the humanistic theology of the liberal churches, citing the failure of secular humanism to provide vision or motive for the creation of the future society that we have told them is their task.

On the other hand, those whose experiences in the counterculture led them into Eastern religions or psychological movements of personal development have offered new definitions of sanctification as enlightenment or self-actualization. Again, the question arises as to the way such salvation may be translated into socially relevant forms. Alumni of these movements are also coming to the churches and the seminaries in search of ways to tie their new insights into social processes that can make them applicable to more persons than themselves.

Finally, those who found primary meaning in the establishment of caring communities are showing signs of having discovered the limits of community within a single age group and seek churches where they can relate across the generations in the kind of loving care they had not found in the neighborhoods of their mobile childhood.

Some of the historic sects offered all three functions that are now being sought. Those that claimed a transcendent God who ruled history, who was the author of personal salvation, were most able to develop over time into main-line denominations, accepting social responsibility as institutions. They offered specific training in spirituality that contributed to the development of relatively secure and positive personalities. They did this in the context of a community of believers that offered support, admonition, and structure to their members. Out of such communities and such forms of personal development they were able to send forth effective people who had motivation to spend their lives in the pursuit of the public good and who had a grounded hope that their efforts would not be in vain.

Main-line churches, whether or not their roots were in sectarian groups, have been able to move beyond the simple motivation of individuals to be responsible for their fellow human beings, to providing channels through which that responsibility could be exercised. Their works of corporate charity, community betterment, their activities as a conscience of the society, should not be forgotten. But in recent years these have become muted in the dual streams of pluralism and special interest that have made the churches suspect. Do they indeed represent universal values and general interests? It is in that question that we find the demand for cultural reconstruction coming out of the ashes of the counterculture. In this age the churches may or may not be the instruments of social reform. They have a vested interest in things as they are, which makes it more difficult for them to envision a different society. For this, they surely are the subjects of reform. Perhaps if religious reform is successful, it can indeed be the channel of a wider reconstruction of the culture, which is the task given to the Vietnam generation but really the responsibility of all of us. Can we learn a lesson from those earlier sects that participated in the formation of the society in those earlier areas of dislocation on the frontier?

One thing we have noted, and which seems to have been a demand of the countercultural experiment, has to do with a theology that takes seriously a sense of the divine, of a transcendent or ultimate dimension of human life, that recognizes mystery and takes seriously the limits of human reason. A society that dwells on the edge of a space age where quantum physics, concepts of antimatter and black holes, all the ramifications of Einsteinian physics that defy ordinary logic, must be willing to free its consciousness from rigid definitions of rationality. A culture that recognizes the importance of the nonrational in the human psyche and in social processes need not reject out of hand religious traditions on the basis of their apparent lack of rationality. There may be new bases of reason out there to explore. How strange if the social institution most identified with the ineffable experience of the holy should be the last to recognize this! Surely we need to bring all the insights of a long tradition of religious experience to a society that has no idea how to handle the dimensions of awe and mystery, or else they may become new prisons we make for ourselves in belief structures that try to contain the uncontainable. Certainly at a time when we are stepping out into unfamiliar ground in so many aspects of life, that portion of our culture which contains all the best insights of our heritage about the ultimate nature and destiny of ourselves and our world needs to be made visible and accessible. Without hope, the new is a paralyzing threat. For those grounded in a world view that posits an ultimate purpose to human activity, the new is an exhilarating challenge. So it would seem that the times demand of the churches a theology unafraid to project beyond the known, to speak of the ultimate in more explicit language than may have been popular in recent years, but also to do so in responsible ways, rescuing religious experience from the realm of experiment and thrill.

At the same time, the interest in Eastern and other religions unfamiliar to our society reminds us that a world made small by modern communications and travel cannot long tolerate a vision of divine purpose limited to one particular class or nation. The rise of a chauvinistic Islam may indeed tempt us to respond in kind; yet our dismay at this manifestation of nationalistic religion should serve as a reminder of its inappropriateness for ourselves as well. It calls us to reexamine the assumptions of our civil religion in the light of universal values. The new world we declared to be the inheritance of the Vietnam generation cannot survive in a welter of particularistic visions of its nature. In fact, this is only an explicit example of that baptism by religious groups of single issue politics that must be transcended by responsible public participation. We are called to evaluate such political narrowness on both the domestic and the international scene, to be responsible to more than our own vested interests.

That sense of responsibility can only be created among people whose vision includes not only a hopeful future but also one in which they have a part. This implies a sense of personal competence and wholeness that must include not only reasonable social and economic skills but also a way of coming to understand oneself as present on the sacred landscape. It is the task of religious groups to provide training in what has traditionally been called "spirituality"—an introduction not only to the history and traditions of the faith but also explicit direction in practices of meditation or prayer, study, and contemplation, in which a person can stand back from everyday pursuits and practice a different perspective in which those activities do not encompass all of ultimate reality. Spiritual disciplines, if they accomplish this, are modes of personal freedom, of moving beyond the present into higher possibilities. Only a person who is free to think beyond the daily tasks of life can have anything to offer others. It is here that we find the sources of hope and motivation that tie the individual into the larger vision of a better society.

But the larger picture is never meaningful if it is only visionary. It must also be experiential. The individual learns to make use of insights gained through spiritual disciplines only in a community of others who can take those insights seriously. Shared visions are the source of cultural revitalization. Part of the grounding of such visions in human community rests in the sense of direction that can come from contact with the past. Only when we know where we have come from are we able to judge where it is we are going. In human society we get that perspective from those who are older, who have lived through earlier manifestations of the culture and so have some idea of the trajectories of change. One reason for the failure of the counterculture may well have been its lack of a sense of direction that came from having no contact with older generations. In modern society we have tended to isolate the old almost as much as the young in patterns of housing, of work, and of recreation. One of the few places where three or more generations are in contact is in the churches, though the opportunity for creative dialogue among the generations is rarely exploited.

Ideally, then, the churches are the institutions of modern society most capable both of bringing the dislocated generation back into contact with the rest of society and of making that contact fruitful in a mutual acceptance of the task of adapting our culture to its times. In the intergenerational community of the church it is possible to put a human face on our understanding of where we have been and where we seem to be heading, so that it becomes more clear how much adjustment in our direction is necessary, what out of the past is worth keeping or restoring, how much of the present could remain within a positive trajectory. In the religious fellowship we live among those who have faith in the future, who hope that it may more nearly reflect a great design that they believe in. In this fellowship the work of change becomes less desperate, more joyful, more a labor of love. In the teaching and practice of the church it should be possible to learn patterns of thinking and behaving that are not dependent upon forms that we suspect are insecure, on their way out.

Ideally, within the fellowship of the church there can be modeled a new definition of the good life, more appropriate for our time, less grounded in those social forms that have proved inadequate and alienating. We can trace this in the history of the church. We may argue whether the early church accepted or tolerated slavery in the society in which it was embedded. But in those persecuted cells of early Christians who were both masters and slaves, rich and poor, there was born a quality of fellowship that would eventually make slavery intolerable. It was the compassion of Christian communities that initiated hospitals, orphanages, settlement houses, and other types of social service that eventually became programs of the secular society. The prophetic witness of the fellowship of concern that is the Christian church at its best has made real the visions of a better society held by people in all ages. It has done so by modeling new and better social relationships and by guiding people who have experienced life in that model to project it outward to the structure of the whole society.

Some Questions for the Churches

The time is upon us to make that kind of witness to the present age. The first area of that witness may need to be within the religious institution itself. A sample of the kind of questions that the churches might begin to ask in relation to their own structure and programs, which might lead to new forms of being in the world, might include the following:

1. One of the most pervasive forms of organization in modern society, also held to be particularly alienating, is that of bureaucracy. At the present time, our churches reflect in their structure the bureaucratic patterns of the society. Is it time for us to examine our organization, from local congregation to national and international systems, to see if there might be alternatives? Could some of the young adults who experimented with alternative communities offer insights? Could older members, who came of age before the bureaucracy was so thoroughly in place, remember other forms that might be revived? Could those now functioning in specialized positions on bureaucratic staff envision other ways to work?

2. How should we relate to the new forms of religiosity, of religious populism in our time? Is it leading the way toward a better future or away from it? Are there elements of this

religiosity that need to be preserved and emulated, elements that need to be discarded?

3. If we are serious about questioning the bases of our rationality in the light of Einstein's universe, are there ways we can reclaim the heritage of mysticism out of which new visions have in the past been sought and found, without falling prey to mere enthusiasm? Can the young, who sought visions in the experiences of the counterculture, provide insights on spiritual disciplines? Can the old, whose training in personal piety was much more explicit than what we know now?

4. Can the churches frame an ethic that makes involvement rather than escape the definition of the good life? Or, indeed, is the pace of modern life and its sensory load so great that churches must learn to model an appropriate alternation of involvement and recreation that is more than escape? Are there, for example, real possibilities in the techniques of meditation and contemplation made visible in the counterculture, by which we could both express our heritage of piety *and* cope with the pressures of modern society? What are the relationships between Christian asceticism, meditation, and such current enthusiasms as jogging?

5. If the churches take seriously the notion that public responsibility is part of the Christian task of loving one's neighbor, how can they engage in equipping people for that task? Can they help to shape an identity in persons that includes a genuine appropriation of public roles as part of the self? Can they offer channels of involvement in the society where those roles may be both accepted as part of the life of the Christian community and supported as they reach beyond its bounds?

6. What are the experiences of human life, personal and corporate, that we need to be providing today's children, so that they as individuals and the society in which they live may reach their full potential? In what ways may their families, however they have experienced them, become part of the universal family of God? What kind of education will they need, and what portion of it should be expected of the churches and in what form? Must we help these offspring of a gen-

eration that has been dislocated to find a place for themselves in the public process that their parents may never find?

Answers to such questions may begin to define the contours of a religion that could both bring a dislocated generation back into constructive social location and being and to address some of the issues that created their dislocation in the first place. If that generation remains dislocated or if those problems are not addressed, it may be difficult for the society to maintain itself in the ordinary way by shaping each new generation to take up where the old one must of necessity leave off. The discontinuities in the pattern of incorporating the young into this ongoing process which came to a peak in the lives of the generation that came of age during the Vietnam war are likely to be too great to be bridged without agony by the generations that follow. Without patterns of this sort a society may only sustain itself by force, and eventually even the instruments of force, the police and the military, collapse if their recruits have no stake in the society. Thus creating new patterns or mending old ones becomes an issue of social and cultural survival no less critical than problems of war or economic sufficiency.

One of the primary means of engaging new generations in the processes of social life has been their socialization into common values and a world view that provides some hope of ultimate purpose in human life, individual and corporate. While socialization is something that occurs in all facets of a person's life, it has been the religious institution that has most explicitly dealt with values and ultimate purpose. Thus the religious institution is faced with taking responsibility for aiding in the relocation of dislocated generations unless it wishes to see itself replaced by other, perhaps less hopeful, agencies or to stand by and watch the collapse of the society. It will not be enough, as we move toward a new millennium of human history, for churches simply to minister to those who are already present in their programs. They must engage these other issues, or they will have been unfaithful stewards of the message they claim to be "Good News."

Notes

Chapter 1

[1] See Margaret Mead, *Culture and Commitment: A Study of the Generation Gap* (New York: Doubleday & Co., Inc., 1970).

[2] Charles Y. Glock and Robert Wuthnow, "The Religious Dimension: A Report on Its Status in a Cosmopolitan American Community" (Paper presented at the International Symposium on Belief, Baden bei/Vienna, Austria, January 8-10, 1975).

[3] Oscar Handlin, *The Uprooted*, 2d ed. (Boston: Little, Brown & Company, Inc., 1973), pp. 231-254.

[4] David Riesman, *The Lonely Crowd* (New Haven: Yale University Press, 1950).

[5] Cf. William H. Whyte, Jr., *The Organization Man* (New York: Simon & Schuster, Inc., 1956), Riesman, *op. cit.*, and Sloan Wilson, *The Man in the Gray Flannel Suit* (New York: Simon & Schuster, Inc., 1955). This last book was also made into a popular movie.

[6] Gibson Winter, *The Suburban Captivity of the Churches* (New York: Doubleday & Co., Inc., 1961).

138   Religion for a Dislocated Generation

⁷Will Herberg, *Protestant-Catholic-Jew* (New York: Doubleday & Co., Inc., 1955).

⁸One example of this was the Faith and Life Curriculum of the Presbyterian Church in the U.S.A., whose elaborately structured program had to be abandoned by the early 1960s because most local congregations found it unworkable. The curriculum, based on a three-year cycle, often used books written by recognized religious scholars and assumed that parents would take responsibility for much of their children's religious education. Few congregations lived up to that expectation.

Chapter 2

¹For a comparison between an American and an English community in this regard, see Roger G. Barker, "Ecology and Motivation," *Nebraska Symposium on Motivation* (1960), pp. 1-48.

²For example, see Peter Berger, Brigitte Berger, and Hansfried Kellner, *The Homeless Mind* (New York: Random House, Inc., 1973).

³As, for example, in his *The Technological Society* (New York: Alfred A. Knopf, Inc., 1964).

⁴"Little Boxes," words and music by Malvina Reynolds. Published by the Schroder Music Company, Berkeley, California.

⁵Theodore Roszak, *The Making of a Counterculture* (New York: Doubleday & Co., Inc., 1969).

⁶William Butler Yeats, *The Second Coming* (New York: Macmillan, Inc., 1924) as quoted in Oscar Williams, ed., *A Little Treasury of Modern Poetry* (New York: Charles Scribner's Sons, 1946), p. 459.

⁷Margaret Mead, *Culture and Commitment: A Study of the Generation Gap* (New York: Doubleday & Co., Inc., 1970).

⁸Daniel Yankelovich, Inc., *The Changing Values on Campus* (New York: Washington Square Press, 1972), chapter 2.

⁹Daniel Yankelovich, *The New Morality* (New York: McGraw-Hill, Inc., 1974), chapter 6.

¹⁰See, for example, Alvin Gouldner, *The Future of Intellectuals and the Rise of the New Class* (New York: The Seabury Press, Inc., 1979).

Chapter 3

¹John B. Orr and F. Patrick Nichelson, *The Radical Suburb* (Philadelphia: The Westminster Press, 1970).

²Harvey Cox, *The Secular City*, rev. ed. (New York: Macmillan, Inc., 1966), pp. 19-32.

³See, for example, Thomas Altizer and William Hamilton, *Radical Theology and the Death of God* (Indianapolis: The Bobbs-Merrill Co., Inc., 1966); Paul van Buren, *The Secular Meaning of the Gospel* (New York: Macmillan, Inc., 1963); and Thomas Altizer, *The Gospel of Christian Atheism* (Philadelphia: The Westminster Press, 1966).

⁴See Peter L. Berger and Thomas Luckmann, *The Social Construction of Reality* (New York: Doubleday & Co., Inc., 1966).

⁵From Leonard Cohen, *Beautiful Losers* (New York: Bantam Books, Inc., 1969), pp. 197-199. Copyright © 1966 by Leonard Cohen. Reprinted by permission of Viking Penguin, Inc. Music may be found on Vanguard Record VSD 79300, *Illuminations*.

⁶Lyrics copyrighted by Almo Music Corporation. Performed on Chrysalis Record CHR 1044, *Aqualung*.

⁷Harvey Cox, *Turning East* (New York: Simon & Schuster, Inc., 1977), particularly chapter 9.

⁸The idea of "mental isolation" is taken from Howard Becker, "Current Sacred-Secular Theory," *Modern Sociological Theory*, ed. Howard Becker and Alvin Boskoff (New York: Holt, Rinehart & Winston, Dryden Press, 1957), chapter 6.

⁹See D. W. Peterson and Armand Mauss, "The Cross and the Commune: An Interpretation of the Jesus People," *Religion in Sociological Perspective*, ed. Charles Y. Glock (Belmont, Calif.: Wadsworth, Inc., 1972).

¹⁰Richard Quebedeaux, *The Young Evangelicals* (New York: Harper & Row, Publishers, Inc., 1974).

¹¹Erik H. Erikson, *Identity: Youth and Crisis* (New York: W. W. Norton & Co., Inc., 1968), pp. 133-134.

¹²Phillip Hammond, *The Campus Clergyman* (New York: Basic Books, Inc., Publishers, 1966), pp. 126-129.

Chapter 4

¹Karl Mannheim, *Essays on the Sociology of Knowledge* (New York: Oxford University Press, Inc., 1952), chapter 7.

²*Ibid.*

³*Ibid.*

⁴Robert Wuthnow, "Recent Patterns of Secularization: A Prob-

lem of Generations?", *American Sociological Review*, vol. 41, no. 5 (October, 1976), p. 858.

⁵ Mannheim, *op. cit.*, p. 310.

⁶ See Marshall McLuhan, *Understanding Media: The Extensions of Man* (New York: McGraw-Hill, Inc., 1964).

⁷ Herbert Marcuse, *One-Dimensional Man* (Boston: Beacon Press, 1964).

⁸ Roszak here was quoting William Blake. For his use of the idea, see Theodore Roszak, *Where the Wasteland Ends: Politics and Transcendence in Post-Industrial Society* (New York: Doubleday & Co., Inc., 1973), pp. 100 ff.

⁹ Jess Moody, *The Jesus Freaks* (Waco, Texas: Word, Inc., 1971), p. 69. The italics are Moody's.

¹⁰ Max Weber, *The Protestant Ethic and the Spirit of Capitalism*, trans. Talcott Parsons (New York: Charles Scribner's Sons, 1930). See also Max Weber, *From Max Weber: Essays in Sociology*, ed. Hans Gerth and C. Wright Mills (New York: Oxford University Press, Inc., 1958), pp. 302-322.

¹¹ Robert Wuthnow, *Experimentation in American Religion* (Berkeley: University of California Press, 1978), p. 196. His quote is taken from William Kornhauser, *The Politics of Mass Society* (New York: The Free Press, 1959), p. 103.

¹² Dean Kelley, *Why Conservative Churches Are Growing* (New York: Harper & Row, Publishers, Inc., 1972).

¹³ Ronald Inglehart, *The Silent Revolution* (Princeton: Princeton University Press, 1977).

¹⁴ See, for example, James T. Richardson, Mary Harder, and R. B. Simonds, *Organized Miracles* (New Brunswick, N.J.: Transaction Books, 1979).

¹⁵ Roy Wallis, *The Road to Total Freedom* (New York: Columbia University Press, 1977).

Chapter 5

¹ Will Herberg, *Protestant-Catholic-Jew* (New York: Doubleday & Co., Inc., 1955).

² H. Richard Niebuhr, *Christ and Culture* (New York: Harper & Row, Publishers, Inc., 1951).

[3] Horace Sutton, "80s Traveler: His Life and Future Times," *Saturday Review* (January 5, 1980), p. 24.

[4] Ernst Troeltsch, *The Social Teaching of the Christian Churches*, trans. Olive Wyon, 2 vols. (New York: Harper & Row, Publishers, Inc., 1960), vol. 1, chapter 2.